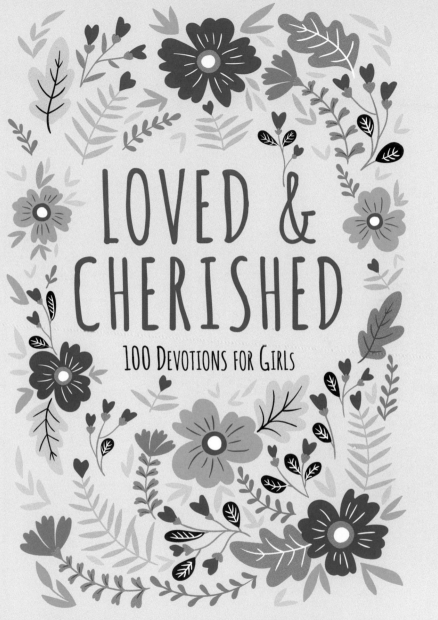

LOVED & CHERISHED

100 Devotions for Girls

LYNN COWELL & MICHELLE NIETERT, M.A., LPC-S, CSC

Z | ZONDERkidz

ZONDERKIDZ

Loved and Cherished
Copyright © 2020 by Lynn Cowell and Michelle Nietert

Requests for information should be addressed to:
Zonderkidz, *3900 Sparks Dr. SE, Grand Rapids, Michigan 49546*

ISBN 978-0-310-76997-2 (hardcover)

ISBN 978-0-310-76998-9 (ebook)

Library of Congress Cataloging-in-Publication Data

Lynn Cowell is represented by the literary agency of The Fedd Agency, Inc., Post Office Box 34193, Austin, Texas 78734.

Michelle Nietert is represented by the literary agency of The Blythe Daniel Agency Inc., Post Office Box 64197, Colorado Springs, CO 80962.

Zonderkidz is a trademark of Zondervan.

Zondervan titles may be purchased in bulk for educational, business, fundraising, or sales promotional use. For information, please email SpecialMarkets@Zondervan.com.

Cover Design: Band Navigation
Interior Design: Denise Froehlich

Printed in China

22 23 24 LEO 10 9 8 7 6 5 4 3

To my delightful, talented, God-seeking daughter Sophia. May you hold tight to the love of God you know and may it grow in and through you as each day of your life passes. You are the child I begged God for and He gave me, in you, a gift beyond what I could have asked or imagined.

Love you to the moon and back, Mom

To Abigail and Emma,

With Love, Aunt Lynn

CONTENTS

SECTION 1: I AM LOVED

SECTION 2: I AM CHERISHED

SECTION 3: I AM SECURE

INTRODUCTION

Hi, Friend!

I'm Lynn! I'm so excited you've decided to join me in discovering God's love! I've been on this journey for a while and do you want to know a secret? The more I learn about how much God loves me, the more I love *me*! My confidence grows as I discover just how deeply I am loved and how much I am cherished.

Over the years, I've had a lot of questions about God's love. And trying to figure out the meaning of love by myself hasn't always gone so well. I didn't come up with the right answers. I thought the amount of love God had for me depended on how often I got it right. If I was doing good, His love went up. If I messed up, His love went down. (I can see this type of love in people around me, so God must be that way too, I thought.) I didn't understand God's love—how deep, wide, and perfect it is. He couldn't love me any more than He did right then or does right now!

I think that if I had understood His love better, I would have felt a lot better about myself as I got older. Maybe I wouldn't have struggled so hard to be perfect and get everything right. Just knowing that God loved me no matter what would have relieved a lot of pressure.

That's why I wrote *Loved & Cherished* for you! I want you to know *now* just how crazy God is for you so you can become the best version of yourself!

I've invited my friend, Michelle, to join us on this journey as well.

Hi! I'm Michelle!

I'm so excited to join you and Lynn as we all learn and remember how much God loves us and that He loves us more than we could ever imagine. I have been a school counselor and now have my own counseling office. Sometimes girls come talk to me about how they feel about love and not feeling loved. I am so thankful each one of us has God, who loves us like no one on Earth ever could. I'm excited to get started, aren't you?

Let's go!

HOW TO USE *LOVED & CHERISHED*

STEP 1: READ

Each day, you'll find a new devotion with a Bible verse at the very beginning. Read the devotion but take your time! Let God speak to you through the words on each page. If something interesting stands out, grab a pen or highlighter and mark it to remember!

STEP 2: REFLECT

When you've finished the devotion for the day, you'll see a section called "Living Cherished." This part will help you apply what you read to your own life. It might ask you a question or offer a thought to think on for the day. If you can't answer the question right away, that's OK! Come back to it when you're ready.

STEP 3: PRAY

After you've completed the "Living Cherished" section, you'll find another section called "Talking with God." After all, that's what prayer is, right? This section includes a prewritten prayer that you can pray today. If you feel led to pray more than what's written on the page, go for it! This section is to help you grow confident in talking with God each day.

11

STEP 4: MEMORIZE SCRIPTURE

At the beginning of each section (on pages 13, 79, 147) you'll see a page called "Meditation Matters." Meditation is simply thinking about something. So when we meditate, or think about Scripture, it's a really cool way for us to connect with God! You can refer back to these pages at the end of each day to read, meditate, and try to memorize Scripture.

SECTION 1

I AM LOVED

Meditation Matters Verses

"Praise the LORD! He is good. God's love never fails."

PSALM 136:1 CEV

"And so we know and rely on the love God has for us. God is love. Whoever lives in love lives in God, and God in them."

1 JOHN 4:16 NIV

"The LORD appeared to us in the past, saying: "I have loved you with an everlasting love; I have drawn you with unfailing kindness."

JEREMIAH 31:3 NIV

LOVED FROM THE VERY BEGINNING

LYNN

So God created humans to be like himself; he made men and women.

GENESIS 1:27 CEV

I wish you and I could go get ice cream together and hang out. (That is if you love ice cream as much as I do!) I'd ask about when and where you were born so I could learn about the very beginning of *you*.

Have you ever thought about why you were created? Well, from the very first verse of the very first book of the Bible, we get a glimpse into why God created you and me. Let's read a few verses from Genesis to find out more!

Genesis 1:1 tells us, "In the beginning, God created . . ." Later in Genesis 1:26 (NLT) it says "Then God said, 'Let us make human beings in our image, to be like us . . .'" The *us* in this verse is God the Father, Jesus the Son, and the Holy Spirit; the whole God family was there. *This* is the family we have been born into. Yes, from the very beginning, we have been invited to belong to God's family. When we were created, God opened the doors of His family wide to us all; for this perfect God loves everybody. That is why we were created. We were created because this loving God had so much love to share He wanted to share it with you and me. That is how John 3:16 starts out, "For God so loved the world . . ."

14

From the very beginning—the beginning of the world and the beginning of your life—you have been loved. Treasured. Adored. Cherished. Wanted. Prized.

I know that is not the message you get day in and day out in this sometimes lonely and often very hard world. In fact, lots of days it feels just the opposite! Maybe you feel disliked, abandoned, ignored, invisible, forgotten, or unwanted. Those feelings, while they are very real and valid, are not the truth. But, boy, they sure can be believable when your teacher comes down on you, your friend fights with you, or your parent is disappointed in you.

I'm so glad that we can look to God's Word to know what He says because in the end, what our Creator says about what He has created is most important!

LIVING CHERISHED

Circle the words that best describe how you are feeling today: **Treasured. Disliked. Adored. Abandoned. Cherished. Ignored. Wanted. Invisible. Prized.** Don't see the word that describes how you are feeling? Write your own list in the lines below. Now, talk to God about how you feel and what you are learning about what He says. The prayer prompt in the next section will help you get started.

....

....

....

TALKING WITH GOD

God, thank You for Your love for me. Thank You that I can talk to You about how I feel. Today, I feel _____. No matter how I feel today—good or bad, happy or sad—You still love me. In Jesus' name, amen.

DAY 2

WHO ARE YOU?

Lynn

I in them and you in me—so that they may be brought to complete unity. Then the world will know that you sent me and have loved them even as you have loved me.

JOHN 17:23 NIV

What words would you use to describe yourself? Some days you might answer with a list of all kinds of good words. *Funny, kind, generous, joyful, helpful, patient.* But other days . . . not so much. The way we feel about ourselves can go up and down faster than that roller coaster you bravely hopped on last summer!

I don't know about you, but for me, that whole up-and-down thing is exhausting. Feeling great about myself one day and crummy the next isn't fun at all. But what is a girl to do when her feelings shove her around like that? Feelings are so powerful, and very convincing too!

While we can't pretend feelings don't exist, I don't want them to control my life. When I'm feeling sad, mad, happy, angry, or fearful, I want to know that underneath all my feelings, there is also truth that I can hang onto. Truth I can tell my heart so that I am not stuck in my feelings.

That truth is: No matter what happens to me today and no matter what comes my way, I am loved. Period. I am crazy, madly, overwhelmingly loved by God. And His love for me is bigger than any feelings that try to control me.

16

In John 17:23 (NIV), Jesus is talking to Father God and He says, "Then the world will know that you sent me and have loved them even as you have loved me." God loves you as much as He loves Jesus. *Isn't that simply amazing?*

It might take us a while to grasp just how deep, unconditional, and perfect this love of God is. I mean, we've never seen anything like it before. So let's keep reading His word so our hearts and minds can take in this truth and believe it!

LIVING CHERISHED

Say out loud: "God loves me just like He loves Jesus. And His love for me is bigger than the feelings that try to control me." Now write down some ways you can remind yourself that you are so loved!

....

....

....

TALKING WITH GOD

God, Your love really is amazing. Thank You for loving me on my good days and bad days, and for helping me overcome my negative feelings. In Jesus' name, amen.

GOD THOUGHT OF YOU BEFORE THE BEGINNING

LYNN

Even before he made the world, God loved us and chose us in Christ to be holy and without fault in his eyes.

EPHESIANS 1:4 NLT

How big is your imagination? Let's find out! Close your eyes and think about what the universe might have looked like before there was . . . anything. What a huge concept!

In this space, before the beginning, even before the world was made, Ephesians 1:4 tells us God loved and chose you! Even then, His love motivated Him as He made His plans to create you and then send His son Jesus, to come for you.

One thing I absolutely love is getting a gift that shows someone thought about me way ahead of time. To me, their planning ahead says, "I love you so much, I thought of you early!" It says that they did the work before my birthday to dream up something they thought I would like; a gift or time together that would show me how much I am loved.

God did that and more for you. God planned ahead! He picked you; He chose you. He chose you even though He knew you would sin or mess up. But you know what? He doesn't want to leave you the way you are!

Jesus' death on the cross for us, erasing our sins, means

that we can be without fault in His eyes. Blameless, faultless, perfect; that is what God sees when He looks at us. Not because *we* don't fail, but because *Jesus* never fails. When God looks at us, He sees what Jesus has done for us by dying to take away all our sins. His perfection makes us right in God's eyes.

LIVING CHERISHED

Are you ready to ask Jesus to take away your sin forever? Ask an adult you trust to help you with this decision! Write about how this decision makes your heart feel. Refer to page 219 in the back of the book.

....

....

....

TALKING WITH GOD

God, thank You for planning for me way ahead. Thank You that even before the beginning, You already loved me and chose me. In Jesus' name, amen.

DAY 4

YOU HAVE HIS NAME

LYNN

*Now I am departing from the world; they are
staying in this world, but I am coming to you.
Holy Father, you have given me your name; now
protect them by the power of your name so that
they will be united just as we are.*

JOHN 17:11 NLT

On a steamy summer day in July, I was born into a family;
a big family that already had six kids *before* I came along!
The day I was born, I was given the last name Martin. It was
my dad's name and the name my mother took when she married Dad. I left that hospital as Lynnette Marie Martin.

What's your full name? Write it here: _____

Your name may say you belong to your dad's family, your
mom's family, or the wonderful family that adopted you and
chose to make you theirs.

Did you know you have another name? This one is even
more important than the name that follows your first name.
This name is: God's daughter. Here is the very cool thing—If
you've said "yes" to becoming a part of God's family, you and I
have the *same* name!

In John 17, Jesus is having a conversation with His father,
God. Jesus, God's son, is getting ready to leave the earth and
head back to His home in heaven with God. He says in verse 11
(NIV), "I will remain in the world no longer, but they are still in
the world, and I am coming to you. Holy Father, protect them

by the power of your name, the name you gave me, so that they may be one as we are one."

This verse tells us that Jesus and Father God share the same name. We—you and me—also have the same name as *that* family; the family of Father God, Jesus, and the Holy Spirit. You and I are a part of this perfect, holy family. We are God's daughters and Jesus' sisters. This incredible privilege was given to us the day we said "yes" to being in the Family. We were given a new name on that day: Father God's family name.

So, whether you are proud of the name at the end of your signature or wish it was a different one and that you belong to a different earthly family, hold this truth close in your heart: your last name—the one saying who you belong to—that name is Father God's. You are His!

LIVING CHERISHED

Try to picture what it is like to be a part of this great big family! Close your eyes and picture heaven, filled with all different colors, shapes, and sizes of brothers and sisters with Jesus and the Father standing by. Describe or draw it below.

....

....

....

TALKING WITH GOD

Father, thank You for giving me Your name. What a concept, that I am in the same family as You, Jesus, and the Holy Spirit. Thank You for choosing me and for this beautiful gift of being Yours. In Jesus' name, amen.

WE ARE FAMILY!

MICHELLE

Yet to all who did receive him, to those who believed in his name, he gave the right to become children of God—children born not of natural descent, nor of human decision or a husband's will, but born of God.

JOHN 1:12–13 NIV

M*y family stinks!*
      I love my family!

Have you ever thought or said both of these phrases within a short period of time? I sure have. When we were doing something fun and my parents were in a good mood, I loved being in my family. When I fought with a brother or sister, had to do chores, or my parents yelled at me, I wanted out.

No matter the family we are born into, the Bible says that because we are adopted as God's kids we have a bigger family than the one we live with every day. This makes life better when we feel like people in our own family aren't that great or are so involved in their own problems, they seem like they've forgotten about us, doesn't it?

When someone adopts you, it legally means you are theirs forever. The cool thing about being adopted by God is that He is a perfect parent and can do more than our earthly parents ever could. He is always available, never distracted, ready to listen, always patient and gentle with us . . . even if we are having the worst day ever.

The next time you get in trouble or are alone and wish your family loved you more or was more like someone else's, turn to God, your forever parent. Tell Him about it. He will be there ready and listening. You are His kid and He cares about you and what's happening in your life and family. Some families are amazing and some are really hard to live with. I get it. So does He.

Also, I want to challenge you to find another grown-up to talk to when life is hard and your parents may be busy. When I taught school and worked as a school counselor, I got to listen to lots of kids' problems. God often uses people who are part of His huge family to provide the love, attention, and encouragement each one of us longs for every day.

LIVING CHERISHED

Make a list of three grown-ups you can talk to if you need help.

....

....

....

TALKING WITH GOD

Father, thanks for making me part of Your huge family. Help me to remember that even when no one else seems to care, You are listening. In Jesus' name, amen.

THE TRUE YOU

LYNN

Some, however, did receive him and believed in him; so he gave them the right to become God's children. They did not become God's children by natural means, that is, by being born as the children of a human father; God himself was their Father.

JOHN 1:12–13 GNT

Have you heard the phrase "just be yourself?" It can be hard to know who our true self really is, especially when there is a lot of change happening in our lives.

Sometimes, in fact, I have wondered: *Who is the true me?* Maybe you can relate.

Why is this so hard? Shouldn't it be simple to know our own personality or the way that we are wired?

If you are a bit like me, the problem with being *the true you* is the thought what if others don't like that you? What if they don't like me? Then the true you doesn't feel like such a great girl.

Today, when I read my Bible, it was one of those WOW kinds of days. I read John 1:13 (MSG): "But whoever did want him, who believed he was who he claimed and would do what he said, He made to be their true selves, their child-of-God selves."

Jesus does the most amazing things! This verse tells us that He gives the gift of becoming His children to those of us who want Him and show that we want the life He offers us by believing He is God's son. He makes us His. Being His is our true self.

If we want to know who we really are, the place to start is by knowing who we are as a child of God. There is a strength, a support, and a steadiness that comes when we know we are His. This verse reassures us that we were not born on this planet simply because two people had a baby. No, we were born to know God as our father and be part of His family.

To be loved like this, by the God of the universe, brings courage to my heart to be the girl I was designed to be by this loving father. If I'm a bit different from others, that makes no difference in God's love for me. He loves me and He made me just the way I am.

This is how you can be the true you . . . loved and cherished.

LIVING CHERISHED

What are three words you would use to describe the *true you*? Are you comfortable being this girl?

....

....

....

TALKING WITH GOD

Father God, thank You for giving me the opportunity to receive You and believe in You, and for making me Your child. I am so very glad to be Yours. In Jesus' name, amen.

GOD, THE ULTIMATE FATHER

LYNN

*So in Christ Jesus you are all children
of God through faith.*
GALATIANS 3:26 NIV

The more I was around my dad, the more I wanted to be around him. I wanted to learn more about who he was simply because he was my dad.

As daughters, we crave knowing our dads and being known by our dads. My dad worked really long days. He went to work before I woke up and often came home after I had gone to bed. Having a dad who worked a lot meant I didn't get to spend much time with him.

Maybe the same is true for you; your dad travels a lot for business, doesn't live with you, lives in a different city, or maybe you don't know who your dad is. That is very hard, especially if you see other girls spending time learning more about their dads. It is hard to get to know a dad who isn't around.

Right now if you don't know your dad very well, you might feel discouraged. I don't want to just brush by this so I want to share some good news with you! God is the ultimate Father who is *always* there, even if your earthly dad might not be. Isn't that amazing? I know it has comforted my heart when it has been hurting.

God wants every person to be in His family, and He invites you to join! He makes it clear *how* we get into His family: "You are all sons of God through faith in Christ Jesus" (Galatians 3:26 NIV).

To become a part of God's family, we have faith in Jesus; to believe and trust in Him.

Being His child doesn't mean we just think that some of the facts about God are true, but that we choose to have a relationship with Him. We make a choice that from now on, Father God is the one who is going to decide what I do with my life. We do this because we believe He knows and will do what is best for us.

I know that right now that may seem hard to do; maybe even overwhelming. As we spend this time together, I hope that you will come to see we can believe God, just how good He really is, because He is trustworthy.

LIVING CHERISHED

Think of how you feel knowing that you are a daughter of God. Describe this feeling below.

....

....

....

TALKING WITH GOD

Father, thank You for giving me the opportunity to get to know You. I want to seek You and find You. Help me to do that with all my heart. In Jesus' name, amen.

I DON'T ALWAYS UNDERSTAND GOD

LYNN

"How can someone be born when they are old?" Nicodemus asked. "Surely they cannot enter a second time into their mother's womb to be born!"

JOHN 3:4 NIV

There is this guy in the Bible that I really like because, honestly, we have a few things in common. One of them is not understanding everything Jesus says.

In John 3, Nicodemus, a guy who was part of the Jewish government, comes to Jesus at nighttime with some questions. I'm not sure why Nicodemus came at night. Maybe he was afraid people would see him with Jesus, and Jesus wasn't too popular at this point. Who knows. (That is just how it is sometimes when we read the Bible. We just don't know everything there is to know.)

When Nicodemus comes to Jesus, he is trying to figure out exactly who Jesus is. Nicodemus knows that Jesus is a teacher and that He has performed some miracles, but he is having a hard time getting the whole picture.

I love how patient Jesus is with Nicodemus. He doesn't call him names for not understanding. He isn't annoyed with him for asking questions. In fact, Nicodemus is the one Jesus speaks this famous verse to: "For God so loved the world that he gave his one and only Son, that whoever believes in him shall not perish but have eternal life" (John 3:16 NIV). He tells Nicodemus the most important thing for him to understand—he is loved.

You might be struggling to understand things about God and Jesus. Let me reassure you: this is normal! There is nothing wrong with you. The best thing you can do right now is share these thoughts with an adult you trust so that maybe they can help you to understand the things you don't.

And while you wrestle with your questions, always keep in mind the truth Jesus told Nicodemus: He loves you so very much that He left all that was perfect to come and die for you. That kind of love is a love worth knowing more about!

LIVING CHERISHED

Do you have some questions about God on your mind? What are they? List them here. Make a point to ask an adult you trust to help you get some answers, and write the answers here too.

....

....

....

TALKING WITH GOD

God, sometimes You are hard to understand. But I have hope. I know over time You'll help me get to know You more. Thank You for loving me, even when I don't understand it all. In Jesus' name, amen.

GOD'S SONG FOR YOU

MICHELLE

*The LORD your God is with you, the Mighty
Warrior who saves. He will take great delight
in you; in his love he will no longer rebuke you,
but will rejoice over you with singing.*

ZEPHANIAH 3:17 NIV

My daughter has her very own song that I've sung over her since the first night I brought her home:

> Sophia Marissa, I love you.
> Sophia Marissa, I'll be true.
> Sophia Marissa, no matter what you do,
> Your mama and your daddy will always love . . . you.

Sometimes before I tuck her in or when she's really feeling like we are constantly correcting her, I remind her of these words that tell of my love for her no matter what.

Did you know that God is singing over you too?

You are your Father God's precious baby girl . . . no matter how mature you become! He still delights in you. Think of the way we light up and talk in silly, happy voices when we see a cute baby. That is how our God feels about us no matter how old we get!

Do you wonder how I know this is true? Buried in a book in the first part of the Bible called the Old Testament, a prophet named Zephaniah talks about God singing over us:

"The LORD your God is with you, the Mighty Warrior who saves. He will take great delight in you; in his love he will no longer rebuke you, but will rejoice over you with singing" (Zephaniah 3:17 NIV).

Wow! I wonder what God's voice sounds like when He sings. Is His voice loud or soft? Mellow or strong? It's fun to try to envision what our Father God is like!

LIVING CHERISHED

In the lines below, list a few songs you hear on the radio, your iPod, or maybe even at church that remind you of how much God loves you. Today, sing one of those songs in the shower, on the way to school, or as you go to sleep. For even more fun, make up words and a tune that you'd like to have God singing over you.

....

....

....

TALKING TO GOD

God, it's hard to imagine that You, the God of the universe, have time to sing over one person . . . especially me. Help me to know that You love me that much, and to rest in Your words of delight over me even when I've had a bad day or think I've messed up too much. Help me remember the reason You do so is because of who You are. In Jesus' name, amen.

PROOF OF GOD'S LOVE

LYNN

*For God so loved the world that he gave his
one and only Son, that whoever believes in
him shall not perish but have eternal life.*

JOHN 3:16 NIV

I know. This is a verse you might have already heard. There is a reason why we read, study, and learn John 3:16. It is because this verse sums up God's love in 26 words.

Think of all the ways you use the word "love." When you think about it, you probably use the word "love" to describe how you feel about Sour Patch Kids and then tell your mom that you *love* her.

I might say "I love you!" or "I miss you!" but not really act in ways that prove those words are true. Words are easy to say because saying something doesn't cost us anything. Posting on social media doesn't come with a payment and texting has no price tag. But what about when a friend asks you to hang out with her instead of going to the party her parents won't let her attend? Or saying yes to watching your little brother while your parent has to work instead of going to your friend's? *Caring costs something.* The action shows that the words have true meaning.

When we read this verse, it begins with the words "For God so loved the world . . ." It is setting us up to see the doing behind God's words. They were not and are not empty or worthless words. His caring cost something . . . His son.

". . . that he gave his one and only Son." There is the cost: God gave. To prove His love was deeper than a shallow declaration, God acted. He gave. And He gave what was most costly for Him: His Son.

There will probably be days when you mess up and mess up bad. (At least there have been for me.) Your mind will tell you, "God couldn't love you now. Look at what you have done."

I want to reassure the future you: He already knows about the mess-up and He loves you still. When God sent Jesus, He already knew all of the sin of the entire world; all past sins, all present sins, and all sins to come. And He *still* sent Jesus to die to pay the price for all our sins. He sent Jesus so you and He can have a beautiful life together, here and in heaven.

LIVING CHERISHED

Take a moment to think about and write down what you would be willing to give or do to show your parent, sibling, or best friend just how much you love them. Nothing we can ever do compares to what God has done for us, but it is good for us to reflect on what loving someone really looks like.

....

....

....

TALKING WITH GOD

God, thank You that Your love for me isn't just words. It's easy to say, "I love you," but You gave so much to prove it to me. I am so very grateful. Help me always remember how real and deep Your love is. In Jesus' name, amen.

GOD, STRONG IN YOU

MICHELLE

*For the Spirit God gave us does not
make us timid, but gives us power, love
and self-discipline.*

2 TIMOTHY 1:7 NIV

You've got the power! Do you believe it? If you're reading this, you were created by God to be a woman of influence in your culture. It might not seem like it right now, but it's true!

Think about the things you're good at, things that make you stand out. Maybe you're *really* good at math or science and are asked to tutor other students. Maybe, you're a good team leader and can help everyone stay on track. Or maybe you can solve a puzzle faster than anyone else. All of those really amazing things about you are skills that God will use one day in a bigger way!

But you know what? Sometimes girls get the wrong message when they are young. I know, because I was one of them. I was told and often felt like I was too much. I talked too much, did everything too loud, and asked too many questions. I wanted and liked to be in charge. Sometimes other kids and lots of adults didn't know what to do with me and all my energy.

Now I see how God used those strengths I started developing as a younger girl. I get to be a business owner, public speaker, and leader in the field of faith-based mental health. I'm grateful for my God's power and strength that is at work within me. It gives me the ability to do a lot of things well and often in a time crunch.

Maybe you are feeling like you aren't supposed to be the way you are. I remember a friend once told me people would like me better if I pretended to be a little clueless and quieter. Don't spend another minute trying to be someone you are not. You can be confident that you have been made for specific purposes on this earth and your strength is going to be put to amazing use. I have a daughter a lot like me. She is confident, funny, and an energetic leader. You may be also and feel a little different than some of the girls around you. Hang in there! God's got you and He will use everything in your life today to develop the leader you will become tomorrow.

LIVING CHERISHED

Today, know that God's power is at work in you. Look in the mirror and say to the face looking back, "God made you to be a smart and energetic leader." What are some ways you can display God's power at your school, your church, your home, or other places this week? Write down some ideas below.

....

....

....

TALKING WITH GOD

God, thank You for being strong in me even on days when I feel weak. May I tap into Your power every day, looking for ways to develop my leadership skills so You can use me. In Jesus' name, amen.

IT'S OK TO NOT BE PERFECT

LYNN

There is no fear in love. But perfect love drives out fear, because fear has to do with punishment. The one who fears is not made perfect in love.

1 JOHN 4:18 NIV

Do you ever wish you were perfect? It's what we shoot for in a report card, a music piece we play, or even when we paint our nails. We want it to be just right. No mess-ups!

Working at being perfect can cause a lot of problems. In fact, when I think about my life, I can't really say anything about it, or me, is perfect! I can try so hard to make it that way, but something always seems to go wrong—even if just a little bit.

You know one thing that is absolutely perfect? God's love for you! When we understand, even a little, what this perfect love looks like, it begins to shove fear out of our hearts.

The more you and I understand His love for us, we can begin to relax, not feel anxious about the way things may go! I'm sure it is hard to think this way, but God in us can change the way we see the things in our lives that are not so perfect.

That less-than-perfect report card doesn't have to make you feel worthless. Missing a note in the musical performance? You can see it as learning, not failing. Chipped nails on picture day? Worse things could happen.

Wouldn't you like to give up on trying to be perfect?

What if instead of focusing on everything we're not good at or what we've messed up, we start noticing what God helps us do well? And when we do mess up, let's show ourselves some grace and trust that because God made us, we are loved and cherished exactly as we are.

LIVING CHERISHED

What is one area in your life where you are not perfect? Write down a prayer thanking God for your imperfections and asking Him to help you accept your weaknesses.

....

....

....

TALKING WITH GOD

God, thank You for loving me as I am, imperfections and all. Help me remember this truth the next time I'm tempted to make a big deal out of my imperfections. In Jesus' name, amen.

YOU BELONG TO HIM

LYNN

But now in Christ Jesus you who once were far away have been brought near by the blood of Christ.

EPHESIANS 2:13 NIV

I recently had one of "those days." You know, those days when you'd rather go back to bed, pull the covers over your head, and just stay there. I bet you've had a day or two like that!

On those days, when I feel sad, I choose to talk to God. I choose to talk to Him because He is always available, always there for me, even when I feel alone. And when I talk to Him, I try to remember things I know to be true, like how much He loves me, that I belong to Him, and that He will never leave me.

Whether today my feelings tell me that I am loved and Jesus is with me or whether they lie and tell me I'm on my own and alone, my feelings can never change the truth. Jesus hasn't left me, even when I sometimes can't feel Him. Ephesians 2:13 tells me that even though I may feel a certain way, because Jesus died for me, He is near to me . . . always. His forgiveness for my sins makes that possible.

So on the hard days, when my emotions try to push me down, I can choose to remind my heart of the truth—I belong to Jesus and *nothing* can change that.

Especially not the way I feel.

LIVING CHERISHED

You belong to Jesus no matter how you feel. If you are feeling sad today, tell Jesus what is happening in your heart and how you need Him to come and help you right now. If you are feeling happy, then thank Him! Write your prayer below.

....

....

....

TALKING TO GOD

God, thank You for sending Jesus to die for my sins so that I can be near You. Because You forgive me for my sin, nothing can push me away from You, not even my pushy feelings. In Jesus' name, amen.

YOU ARE CHOSEN

Michelle

But you are a chosen people, a royal priesthood,
a holy nation, God's special possession, that you
may declare the praises of him who called you
out of darkness into his wonderful light.

1 PETER 2:9 NIV

"Did you make it?"

This is the first thing I said to my girl when picking her up from school recently. She was at a new school and was trying out for a competition called Oral Reading. Schools give you chances to learn new skills but unfortunately sometimes you have to "make it" in order to get that new opportunity. For those who are chosen, it's an exciting moment. Sophia skipped out of school with a big grin (so I was relieved she "made it"), but I noticed there were other kids walking toward their cars with their heads down, looking sad.

Maybe you've had a moment where you "made it" like Sophia. And maybe you've had a moment where you didn't "make it" and it left you feeling sad too.

Did you know that no matter what happens at a competition, contest, or even with a group of friends, you can be confident knowing you're already forever chosen? There is a verse in the Bible that says God chose you, and when he did it was *forever*. So whether you have a good day or bad day, you are chosen. If your team wins or loses, you are chosen. If you get an amazing grade or have to correct your paper, you can never do or say anything to not be God's chosen girl.

Today, I want to encourage you to walk into your day believing that you are chosen. Because when you live as God's chosen girl, you can hold your head high no matter what the day brings. Today practice walking around feeling and seeing yourself as chosen from the time you wake up in the morning until the time you go to bed. God not only has chosen us but often as we look around, we might notice him demonstrating his love through others. Maybe a friend chooses to sit next to you, talk to you, or stand in line with you. Maybe the teacher gives you a special job. Possibly your parent or brother or sister picks you to play with them or do something special.

LIVING CHERISHED

Write down at least three reminders of different ways you have been chosen. This week reread your list every night to remind yourself how chosen and cherished you are in God's eyes.

....

....

....

TALKING WITH GOD

Father, thank You so much for choosing me no matter what. Help me to remember that I am chosen, to walk in that truth throughout my day, and to give me chances to choose others so I can share Your love with them. In Jesus' name, amen.

IT'S A GOOD DAY TO HAVE A GOOD DAY

LYNN

This is the day that the LORD has made;
let us rejoice and be glad in it.

PSALM 118:24 ESV

Do you ever have songs pop into your head, songs you haven't thought of in a long time?

When I was your age, I was in a children's choir at my church. Being a part of this choir was a wonderful experience and I met people that I still have as friends today!

One of the songs we learned had lyrics right from this verse in Psalm 118:24. "This is the day that the LORD has made; let us rejoice and be glad in it." Some days when I wake up, my mind starts singing this song. I love when this happens because it reminds me exactly where my thoughts should begin before I even get out of bed.

Every morning when we wake up, it means God has given us the gift of another day! We have another day to live and breathe; a day to love those around us, and another day to give Him praise and glory. Our lives might not be great—in fact, some things might be really hard right now. But God promises to be with us and guide us, and that's enough reason to thank Him for another day to live!

LIVING CHERISHED

As soon as you wake up tomorrow morning, say to yourself: "This is the day the Lord has made!" Then smile as big as you can. No matter how you feel when you wake up, if you direct your mind toward positivity, it will help you feel better and remember that God is with you, guiding you every step of the way. What are some positive thoughts or Bible verses you can use to remind yourself of God's gifts? Write them below.

....

....

....

TALKING TO GOD

God, thank You for the gift of today! Thank You for promising to always be with me. Help me to remember that You're there through all the ups and downs of life. In Jesus' name, amen.

GOD'S LOVE NEVER CHANGES

LYNN

Praise the LORD! He is good. God's love never fails.

PSALM 136:1 CEV

Friendships.

Sometimes they are just plain hard. There needs to be a website with instructions on how to figure out our friends, don't you think?

In 5th grade I wrote in my diary for April 25: "Me and Sonia are not best friends anymore, because Sonia is a little bit sick of me. I wish we were still best friends." Ouch! My heart hurts for my young self. *A little bit sick of me?* That's harsh!

Have you been in a situation similar to mine? Maybe you and a friend were as close as could be and then suddenly . . . you weren't anymore. Maybe you said the wrong thing or she looked at you the wrong way. Or, maybe you liked her crush. Then she said you're done being friends.

There are a lot of reasons that friendships end, and I'm sure you have your own that you're thinking about right now.

But you know what? I'm so thankful that God's care for us doesn't flip flop like feelings from our friends. In Psalm 136:1 David writes: "Praise the LORD! He is good. God's love never fails." That is so good, I think we should read it again: God's love *never* fails!

Never!

We can count on God to love us no matter what. What you do can't change His love for you. What other people do can't change His love for you. Because God is perfect, it means His love for you will never change, never decrease, or be taken away. That is really, really good news!

LIVING CHERISHED

I love music! Listening to music that tells me just how much God loves me always fills my heart. In fact, I have a playlist called "Loved & Cherished" on my music app on my iPhone. In the lines below, start building your own playlist of songs that remind you just how much you're loved by God!

....

....

....

TALKING TO GOD

God, thank You that I can't lose Your love or do anything to make You not love me. Help me love others like You love me today. In Jesus' name, amen.

IS THIS GOOD ENOUGH?

LYNN

He called a little child to him, and placed the child among them. And he said: "Truly I tell you, unless you change and become like little children, you will never enter the kingdom of heaven. Therefore, whoever takes the lowly position of this child is the greatest in the kingdom of heaven."

MATTHEW 18:2–4 NIV

As I go back and read my diary from when I was your age, I see activity after activity—piano recitals, choir solos, and play parts. The words I wrote might tell of an activity, but I know the true meaning behind the words.

Back then I thought that what I did and how well I did it determined how important, or valued, I was. One night, after what I thought was a less than stellar performance, I wrote in my diary: "My piano concert tonight wasn't the greatest, but I guess it is OK."

What I didn't write in my diary was how I felt—I wasn't good enough. Continually afraid of what others would think of me, I wanted to feel important. Performing well made me feel valuable.

Jesus makes it clear—He's not into performances. I'm not saying He doesn't want you to do all of the activities you do, but He does want us to be aware of *why* we do the things we do. We don't have to perform for Him. He just wants us to come to Him.

In Matthew 18, Jesus' followers are asking Him how they can be great in His kingdom. Like me, they had it all wrong. They, too, thought it was about performing. But Jesus wants us to have the heart of a little child who trusts and is tender. Little children are willing to let others help them. Jesus is telling us He doesn't need us to try to impress Him with how good we can be or how we can get everything right. He simply wants us to come to Him, and then follow His lead.

That might feel a little backward, especially when you're trying to grow more and more independent. And yet, here is Jesus saying, "I want you to *want* my help." He is always listening to us and giving us His full attention. He wants us to trust Him with anything and everything, just like a little child would.

LIVING CHERISHED

In the lines below, write down all the hobbies and activities you do. Then honestly ask yourself: Are you trying too hard to perform for others, or even for Jesus? How can you use your activities, skills, and talents to give glory and honor back to God? How can you trust His guidance as you grow and change?

....

....

....

TALKING TO GOD

God, it does seem a little weird that You want me to need You when the point of growing up is to learn to be independent. Thank You that You see me as Your child. Guide me as I'm growing up and teach me to love You with the heart of a child. In Jesus' name, amen.

EYES ON YOU

LYNN

*I will instruct you and teach you in the
way you should go: I will counsel you
with my loving eye on you.*

PSALM 32:8 NIV

Getting someone's attention can be really hard, can't it?
You're in the middle of telling a story about the mean things that kid said to you at lunch today, when your mom's phone rings. Suddenly, she's gone. Something "more important" has come up. Fifteen minutes later, she's back. *"What were you saying?"* She tries to get the conversation rolling again, but now you'd rather not talk about it.

It doesn't matter if it's a parent, teacher, coach, or friend, when someone takes their eyes off you and focuses on something else, it can feel like something or someone else is more important than you. Even when they are listening, but that phone is laying there just waiting to ring or ping, we can feel a bit hesitant—at any time their attention can be gone.

When we talk to God, we always have His full attention! He is lovingly watching what's going on in our lives, just waiting for us to come and tell Him all about it. He is waiting for us to ask Him for His wisdom and what we should do next. He is not going to turn His eyes to someone or something else. He is all into you! We are the most important thing in front of Him.

You know what else? God will never abandon you. He is always with you and always wants the best for you.

LIVING CHERISHED

What feelings do you have when someone is distracted when you are telling them a story? How can you kindly share with this person how important it is to you to have their full attention? Write down some ideas below for talking to this person in love.

....

....

....

TALKING WITH GOD

God, thank You for giving me Your full attention. When others are distracted while I talk to them, I feel _____ _____.
Thank You for loving me by always having Your eyes on me! In Jesus' name, amen.

YOUNG WARRIOR

MICHELLE

*Put on the full armor of God, so that you can
take your stand against the devil's schemes.*
EPHESIANS 6:11 NIV

I feel like my teacher doesn't like me." "That girl always makes fun of me." "I feel like my parents only see what I'm doing wrong." Life can seem like a real battle everywhere you turn. The fight is real. But girl, you are a warrior and have a heavenly armor that not only protects you in every battle but will also empower you to win in the long run.

God's armor isn't heavy and made of metal. It's the belt of truth. Every time you read God's Word and even more when you memorize it, you can use His truth to protect you from embracing the lies we can start believing when people say or do mean things to us. God's truth will remind you who you truly are. It's also the sword of the Spirit. The more you connect with God, allowing His Holy Spirit to live in and work through you, the more empowered you will be to fight against the tough blows the world throws at you sometimes.

When we were dating, my husband taught me to play a video game in which I was this awesome warrior woman with all kinds of weapons. I had so much fun running around that world as a strong female fighter.

Today I was reminded that I am that woman. The more I see myself as a warrior in God's army, the more I will learn to fight my battles and win. Because in the end, Jesus and God ultimately win.

LIVING CHERISHED

Imagine or draw yourself as a female warrior. Read Ephesians 6:10–17. Visualize yourself wearing the weapons God has given you, living every day as a warrior, and allowing God to join you in the battle. How do you feel as you imagine yourself this way? Write it down!

....

....

....

TALKING TO GOD

God, I'm so glad I'm a warrior in Your army. Help me to be strong and trust You when I feel weak or defeated by circumstances in this world. Thank You that You have already won the ultimate battle of life forever. In the end, so will I. In Jesus' name, amen.

YOU BELONG TO GOD

Lynn

> But you belong to God, my dear children. You have already won a victory over those people, because the Spirit who lives in you is greater than the spirit who lives in the world.
>
> 1 JOHN 4:4 NLT

You belong to God.

You might not belong with the cool kids, the team you didn't make, or in the accelerated class at school, but you *do* belong in a way that matters more than any of those.

Yes, you belong to God! This belonging to God gives you a superpower of sorts. Obviously not a superpower like girls in the movies; it's a power even stronger.

You have God Himself living inside you! His power is stronger than any bad feelings we might have from not belonging. It is stronger than the devil and any way that he may choose to try to mess up your life and your relationship with God. His power in us can overcome any thoughts that try to make us feel sad or upset.

Sometimes we might not recognize that He is with us and helping us. The voices of others, as well as our own, can be loud; trying to drown out His voice of strength inside. When this happens to me, I know that I need to get alone and be quiet. I need to read verses like this one in 1 John 4:4 (NIV) and remind my mind and heart, ". . . the one who is in you is greater than the one who is in the world."

It's so important that we know God's Word for ourselves; that we read it over and over again. That way, when we are in the times when our mind, our enemy, or other people come at us, we know what God's Word says about us: we belong to God! He is in us and because He is, we can overcome anything!

LIVING CHERISHED

Imagine yourself in a situation where you feel insecure, hearing negative voices from others and from yourself. Then put God in that picture with His voice saying, "I am with you and we've got this." What are some positive thoughts that arise as you imagine God's presence with you in that situation? Write these thoughts down and refer back to them the next time you feel insecure.

....

....

....

TALKING WITH GOD

God, thank You that Your presence in me is my superpower. In Jesus' name, amen.

WHAT IS LOVE, ANYWAY?

Lynn

But anyone who does not love does not know God, for God is love.

1 JOHN 4:8 NLT

Have you ever had someone say, "I love you," but honest-ly—by the way they treat you—it's hard to believe? I sure have, and I bet you have too. Whether it's a best friend, a family member, or even a parent on their worst days, sometimes people simply don't love us well. It can make a girl not want to be "loved" some days!

I'm not sure about you, but these encounters have some-times left me more confused about what love is. Does this mean you're not allowed to ever get mad or upset with some-one you love? If someone loves you, will they never hurt your feelings or say something mean to you? Does it mean that you will do whatever they want?

This "love" thing can be a bit messy and confusing.

To find out the true definition of love, we need to look to the One who tells us He *is* love: God Himself. In 1 John 4:18 it says, "God is love." Here, the word *loved* means, "to love, esteem, cherish, accept, or prize; to be devoted to."

Isn't that beautiful? This is what it means to be loved by God!

LIVING CHERISHED

Choose at least one person whose positivity makes you feel good and write their name(s) below. What about this person makes you feel positive? Try to spend more time around them this week.

....

....

....

TALKING WITH GOD

God, I am so very thankful that You love me so perfectly! Help me grow more and more in my understanding of Your love. In Jesus' name, amen.

JESUS' LOVE NEVER STOPS

LYNN

". . . but whoever drinks of the water that I will give him will never be thirsty again. The water that I will give him will become in him a spring of water welling up to eternal life."

JOHN 4:14 ESV

My heart sank. I hadn't been invited . . . again. I thought we were friends; good friends even. So why did they leave me out? When they made their plans, why didn't I come to mind? As a tear trickled down my face, my heart was deciding which way I was going to choose. I was really tempted to plop on my floor and let the one little tear become a flood. But then I remembered something better than giving into a pity-party.

Jesus can fill that empty place.

In John 4, Jesus and his friends were exhausted from traveling. Making a stop in a town, the guys went to look for food while Jesus took a seat by a well to get a drink. As he rested, a woman came up to get her own water. Since Jesus was without a bucket to get the water, Jesus asked the woman for a drink.

While it looks like this is a conversation about water and being thirsty, it's not. Jesus came to this spot, at this time, because He knew the woman's heart was thirsty. He arranged His day to show up at the well at the exact time she would be there, because He knew her heart was empty. Only He had exactly what she was truly wanted.

Often, when our own tears well up it's because we're empty

too. We want to belong; to be a part of something. Jesus gets that because He made us this way.

At the well, Jesus says, "But whoever drinks of the water that I will give him will never be thirsty again. The water that I will give him will become in him a spring of water welling up to eternal life" (v. 14). Springs are sources of water that come up from the ground. The water just keeps coming and coming and coming, all by itself. Springs are not like wells that can dry up.

Jesus is our source of love that just keeps coming and coming. His love never dries up or stops. His love, when you allow it, can be a continual source of exactly what you need. Especially on the days when our heart is hurt and empty, He comes filling up our empty place again and again and again.

LIVING CHERISHED

One reason that we read God's Word each day is so that on the really hard days, we have all of the love and truth we need. We don't have to look for it because we have been filling up our hearts with it every day. Do you have a few Bible verses in mind that remind you of God's truth? Write down a few below. If you can't think of any verses, ask a trusted grown-up what their favorite verses are for reminding themselves of God's love and promises.

....

....

....

TALKING WITH GOD

God, thank You that You are the source of love that never goes dry; it flows from You to me over and over again. In Jesus' name, amen.

HE IS GOOD WHEN I AM NOT

LYNN

> For the LORD is good, and his faithful
> love endures forever; his faithfulness,
> through all generations.
>
> PSALM 100:5 CSB

For as long as I can remember, I have wanted to be good and do good. I would say that most of the time I have been successful, but I can't say this has *always* been the case.

What does the word *good* really mean?

Dictionary.com says *good* can mean "better or best."

Have I always been the best I can be? For sure not! But there is One who is good—always. In fact, Psalm 100:5 tells us that the definition of good is God Himself. Wow! "For the LORD is good . . ." His love for us is because of His goodness. His love is better; His love is best. And most of all, His love is faithful and it never ends. It is for forever.

God's love for us goes on and on. Forever and ever and ever. God's love has no end. It will never stop. His unfailing, loyal devotion to us, His kindness, will never quit coming to us and will always be for us.

We can never do anything to cause His love to quit coming because His love is not dependent upon us. His love is formed on the foundation of His perfection and He isn't afraid of our flaws.

That takes so much pressure off me! *It's not about how good I am, but how good He is.*

LIVING CHERISHED

Train your brain by repeating over and over: "I don't have to always be good to be loved by God." In what situations will this reminder be most helpful to you? What are some ways that you can remind yourself of this truth in your everyday life?

....

....

....

TALKING WITH GOD

Lord, thank You that Your love for me is not dependent on me being good, but is based on Your goodness alone. In Jesus' name, amen.

LET IT GO

MICHELLE

*Therefore, since we are surrounded by such
a great cloud of witnesses, let us throw off
everything that hinders and the sin that
so easily entangles. And let us run with
perseverance the race marked out for us.*

HEBREWS 12:1 NIV

I am so not a runner. I remember in my physical education class, I hated running, and still to this day, I prefer to walk. I end up running, though, especially when I am in a hurry. My kids are used to me saying, "Hurry up and get in the car." Sometimes they get frustrated with me because I have to turn around and get something I forgot or take something out of our car to make room for something else. The stuff we need or don't need seems to slow us down.

As you get older, you may be tempted to accumulate more physical stuff in your life. Our loads in life can also be emotional and weigh us down. Negative words someone has said to us or hard things that have happened in our lives, bad choices we keep making or don't let go of can weigh us down. It reminds me of my daughter's backpack that is sometimes just too full. I often remind her that running around with a heavy load isn't good for your back.

And carrying around a heavy heart isn't good for our lives, either.

Life can be like a race, and you know what? I've never seen a track star or marathon runner carrying anything. Why? Because they left it behind so they can move fast.

What is something that's weighing you down today? Maybe it's a bad habit or someone's words you just can't get out of your head. Maybe it's a choice you've made and have hidden that is making your heart feel heavy. We all pick up junk along the road of life. God wants to empower you today to dump the weight you may have been carrying and run lighter and faster. Turn to Him and let it go!

LIVING CHERISHED

In the lines below, write down at least one thing you need to let go of today. Then cross it out, scribble over it, or do something else to remind yourself that you've given that burden to God. Each day this week, if you start to think about what you wrote, remind yourself that it's no longer yours to carry.

....

....

....

TALKING TO GOD

Father, even though I'm still a kid, I've picked up or been handed some junk that is weighing me down. Help me make choices today and every day that free me up to run the race of life well, focusing on You every step of the way. In Jesus' name, amen.

IT'S NOT ALL UP TO ME

LYNN

The LORD appeared to us in the past, saying:
"I have loved you with an everlasting love; I
have drawn you with unfailing kindness."

JEREMIAH 31:3 NIV

When I was growing up, one of the phrases I would hear people in church say was "come to Jesus." There was a part of me that really didn't understand what this meant. When I heard "come to Jesus" I thought it was all up to me. I thought that I had to do the work to come to Him and all the work to stay close to Him too.

I understand more clearly now. Jeremiah 31:3 has helped me. It says, ". . . I have loved you with an everlasting love; I have drawn you with unfailing kindness."

According to God, who is the one doing the work here?

It's the Lord. He is the One who draws us to come to Him. He pulls us to Himself with His everlasting love and unfailing kindness.

Yes, we should go after Jesus with all our heart! But we can also rest from working so hard, knowing that while we are going after Him, He is drawing us closer to His heart.

Thank goodness it's not all up to me!

LIVING CHERISHED

Write a description or draw what it looks like to have God bring you close to Him.

....
....
....

TALKING TO GOD

Lord, thank You that You draw me closer to You. In return, I want to love You and know You more. In Jesus' name, amen.

THANK YOU, GOD

Lynn

Let them give thanks to the LORD for
his unfailing love and his wonderful
deeds for mankind.

PSALM 107:31 NIV

Have you ever slowed down and really paid attention to the prayers you pray? I did recently and discovered something.

I noticed most of my prayer is focused on me asking God *for* something. I ask Him to heal those I love who are sick or to help those who are struggling or having a hard time. I might even ask Him *for* something I need.

Today, in my time with Jesus, I read this verse in Psalm 107:31: "Let them give thanks to the LORD for his unfailing love and his wonderful deeds for mankind." It was almost like it was a new thought for me . . . to thank the Lord for the unfailing love that He gives me day after day.

When we take the time to thank God for His love, it is also a reminder to us just how good His love for us is. Thanking Him not only blesses Him because we are being grateful, but it also helps us remember and focus on what is so very good in our lives: His loyal, devoted love and kindness.

LIVING CHERISHED

On this page, write out at least five things you are thankful for, starting with God's unfailing love for you!

....

....

....

TALKING WITH GOD

Father, thank You for Your steadfast love for me! Thank You for _____. You are so good to me! In Jesus' name, amen.

GOD'S GOT MY FUTURE

LYNN

The LORD is my rock, my fortress and my deliverer; my God is my rock, in whom I take refuge, my shield and the horn of my salvation, my stronghold.

PSALM 18:2 NIV

If I were to ask you to describe your future, what would it look like? In 4th grade, I wanted to be a children's book illustrator. My friend and I were really into drawing pictures, and I thought illustrating a book would be the very best job! We were so into it that her mom let us draw pictures on the walls of her attic just for practice.

What about you? Do you ever think about what you'd like to do, where you'd like to go, or where you'd like to live?

I'm a gal who finds thinking about the future thrilling. But sometimes, thinking about the future is scary and we ask a lot of "what ifs." Like, "What if I live far away from my family one day?" Or "What if _____ happens?" (You fill in the blank.)

I don't know the future, but I have to remind myself that God does. Verses like Psalm 18:2 help me know that whatever the future holds, God's got it, and His love will help me face whatever comes my way!

He is your rock, your safe place, and your deliverer from any rough patches. He is the rock we can stand on when life is rough. He is our protection from danger or trouble—the One who holds every detail together. Even as I write this now, I'm smiling. We can trust our God to carry us and our future in His powerful hand.

LIVING CHERISHED

With a grown-up's help, do an internet image search for the word "fortress," or look up pictures of fortresses in a reference book. Aren't they beautiful? What do all of these buildings have in common?

....
....
....

TALKING WITH GOD

Father, as I look at pictures of fortresses, I picture myself safe within them. No matter what comes my way, You protect me. You are my fortress. In Jesus' name, amen.

WHEN SHOUTING IS GOOD

LYNN

*Shout for joy to the LORD, all the earth.
Worship the LORD with gladness; come
before him with joyful songs.*

PSALM 100:1–2 NIV

I studied my part over and over again until I was ready to go! As part of a children's choir at my church, the special performance began with Psalm 100 spoken by children who had memorized each section.

My part was: "Shout for joy to the LORD, all the earth. Worship the LORD with gladness; come before him with joyful songs" (Psalm 100:1–2). I wanted so badly to get this right when I stood before our church that I repeated it to myself over and over until I could say it without even thinking about it.

Now, many years later, this verse that I memorized when I was 10 years old often comes back to me. In fact, this morning, I woke up with it on my mind. It is a beautiful reminder that this is how we can begin our day, heading in the right direction. Giving praise to God not only gives Him what He deserves, which is all of our praise and worship, but it also sets our mind toward being joyful!

LIVING CHERISHED

Find some Bible verses that speak about being joyful and tell of God's greatness! You can do this several different ways. In the back of my Bible, I have something called a concordance. If you have one, you can look up words like "joy" to find verses that use that word. You can also do a search on the internet for verses that use the word you're looking for. Write down your favorite verses on the lines below and refer back to them often!

....

....

....

TALKING WITH GOD

God, I will shout for joy to You because You are so great and powerful. I will be glad and sing songs of worship to You because I want You to know I am grateful for You today. In Jesus' name, amen.

FAITH THAT MOVES MOUNTAINS

MICHELLE

He replied, "Because you have so little faith.
Truly I tell you, if you have faith as small as a
mustard seed, you can say to this mountain,
'Move from here to there,' and it will move.
Nothing will be impossible for you."

MATTHEW 17:20 NIV

I asked my daughter her favorite Bible verse today and was surprised to learn her answer. "Faith can move mountains" was her reply. *Wow, I am raising a mountain-mover!* I thought to myself.

I bet some of you reading this are mountain-movers too. Lately, I've been working on my physical health because I know how much it affects my mental well-being and energy levels. I've been watching from afar a woman I chose as a mentor in this area. Last month, she and her husband went to Utah and literally climbed mountains over and over again until she had climbed as many feet as you would if you'd climbed Mt. Everest, a huge mountain! She talked about how much they had to prepare for this event. They even hired an expert to prepare them so they wouldn't hurt themselves.

You too can be mountain climbers and movers! It might take some serious faith to make it happen. Someone in the counseling office recently asked me, "How do you grow your faith?" My response: One step and mountain at a time. When you join with God and ask Him to empower you to conquer new things or day after day train yourself to do something, you are practicing a faith that moves mountains.

LIVING CHERISHED

Today, pick a "mountain" you want to climb. Maybe your mountain is to run faster or do push-ups in PE class or on your own. My daughter, even though she doesn't take gymnastics, recently decided to learn to do the splits. Reading faster or learning your math facts so they come easily can definitely be mountains as well. After you've chosen your mountain, draw it and name it. Then create a list of steps that will help you climb this mountain. Ask God to help you start. Keep following the steps so you too can climb and move the mountains you encounter or choose in your life.

....

....

....

TALKING TO GOD

Dear God, please help me believe You can work in and through me to move mountains. Teach me how to have the faith to be a mountain-mover all the days of my life. Thanks for the examples of others who can inspire me to do great things. In Jesus' name, amen.

TELL YOURSELF THE TRUTH

LYNN

We demolish arguments and every pretension that sets itself up against the knowledge of God, and we take captive every thought to make it obedient to Christ.

2 CORINTHIANS 10:5 NIV

Have you ever had a thought pop into your head and wondered where it came from? My friend Julie shared with me that when she was a young girl, she thought her parents and everyone around her didn't love her. They told her they loved her, but for some reason she wouldn't believe it.

These negative thoughts can be very powerful, especially if they hang around in our minds for a long time. The more time we spend thinking about them, the more powerful they become.

So if we feel unloved and we begin to believe that this thought and these feelings are the truth, we will begin to act like girls who are unloved.

That's why 2 Corinthians 10:5 is so powerful! It tells us to pay attention to every thought we think. If that thought isn't the same as the truth in God's word, we must tell that thought to back down. We can't continue to think something like "I am not loved" when God has told us—and continues to tell us—that He loves us so very much.

We replace these thoughts with God's truth. That is why the Scriptures in Meditation Matters are so important. As we get truth in our minds, when untruths appear, we can chase them away by reminding ourselves of God's truths. He loves us so much, He gave us His very best in His son, Jesus.

LIVING CHERISHED

Pay attention to your thoughts today. If you recognize a thought that is negative, don't repeat it over and over in your mind. Tell yourself that it is a lie, then replace that thought with a positive thought, with one of the Meditation Matters verses on page 13, or with some of your other favorite verses about God's truths (list these verses below!).

....

....

....

TALKING WITH GOD

God, thank You for loving me today and always. Help me remember how much You love me when negative thoughts try to tell me otherwise. In Jesus' name, amen.

GOD'S LOVE IS TENDER

LYNN

*Love is patient, love is kind. It does not envy,
it does not boast, it is not proud. It does not
dishonor others, it is not self-seeking, it is not
easily angered, it keeps no record of wrongs.*

1 CORINTHIANS 13:4–5 NIV

I looked up the word "love" in the dictionary today. It said that *love* means "to have a profoundly tender, passionate affection for."

Since God Himself is love, then the love He has for us is very tender. It's so important for us to know and understand who God is and what His love for us is like. 1 Corinthians 13 is known as "the love chapter." This whole section of the Bible tells us what love is like, and since God is love, it tells us what God is like.

We can take this verse and put His name in it:

God is patient and kind. God does not envy; He does not boast and He is not proud. He does not dishonor others. He is not self-seeking (God is not selfish). God is not easily angered, and when we mess up, He doesn't keep score.

We need to remind ourselves of what God is like, especially if our feelings tell us that God is mad at us or He thinks we have done something wrong one too many times. These thoughts are not true!

Our God is love, and our God loves us.

LIVING CHERISHED

Open your Bible to 1 Corinthians 13. Read it out loud. Every time you see the word "love," replace it with "God." What are some things you discover about God when you do this? How does that make you feel?

....

....

....

TALKING WITH GOD

Thank You, God, for loving me. For being tender, kind, and patient with me. I need Your love, and I am grateful for all the ways You show it. In Jesus' name, amen.

DAY 32

ROOTED

LYNN

*I pray that out of his glorious riches he may
strengthen you with power through his Spirit
in your inner being, so that Christ may dwell
in your hearts through faith. And I pray that
you, being rooted and established in love,
may have power, together with all the Lord's
holy people, to grasp how wide and long and
high and deep is the love of Christ.*

EPHESIANS 3:16–18 NIV

When my kids were little, their school had a fundraiser selling flower bulbs; wrinkly, brown bulbs that carried the promise of becoming gorgeous blooms one day.

That was many years ago, and yet each spring, green leaves begin to appear in my garden, then buds. Soon, white daffodils burst open.

The reason these bulbs produce beautiful blooms year after year is because they were planted deep. Down into the rich soil, they are protected from winter weather so they can bloom come spring.

In Ephesians 3:16–17, the writer is praying for us. He's praying that we would become so strong in God's love for us, with roots so deep, that no matter what pulls on us God's love cannot be uprooted. We know that He loves us and nothing can ever change that!

LIVING CHERISHED

Have you ever done any gardening or watched a plant grow? What was it like to watch a wrinkly bulb or tiny seed turn into something beautiful, like a flower, or delicious, like a fruit or vegetable? What are some ways you can "plant" yourself in God's love and put down roots there? (Examples: reading your Bible; picking verses to memorize; praying every day; and more! Write your ideas below.)

....

....

....

TALKING WITH GOD

God, thank You that nothing can remove the roots of Your love from my heart. In Jesus' name, amen.

SECTION 2

I AM CHERISHED

Meditation Matters Verses

"But you are a chosen people, a royal priesthood, a holy nation, God's special possession, that you may declare the praises of him who called you out of darkness into his wonderful light."

1 PETER 2:9 NIV

"Since you are precious and honored in my sight, and because I love you, I will give people in exchange for you, nations in exchange for your life."

ISAIAH 43:4 NIV

"The LORD your God is in your midst, a mighty one who will save; he will rejoice over you with gladness; he will quiet you by his love; he will exult over you with loud singing."

ZEPHANIAH 3:17 ESV

GOD, ME, AND NICKNAMES

Lynn

To them I will give within my temple and its walls a memorial and a name better than sons and daughters; I will give them an everlasting name that will endure forever.

ISAIAH 56:5 NIV

When I was a little girl, my father was not available a lot. Working two jobs to take care of his large family, he simply wasn't home. When Dad was home, I looked for ways to be close to him. To talk to him.

Even to this day, my memory recalls him speaking my name. When I "hear" him, he isn't calling me my given name Lynnette or even the shortened version Lynn. He didn't use a name like daughter. Instead, he is using one of the nicknames he gave me; either Lynnzeretta or Squirt. I loved when Dad called me these names. I'm not sure if it was the tone of voice he used or simply that the names were fun, I just know it was as if my heart was smiling when he said my name. These names made me feel close to him.

In God's word, God often changed people's names. The list is long, including Sarai to Sarah and Saul to Paul. God gave them these new names as they came to know Him in a deeper way. He gave them these names as the two of them became closer.

Just like my dad gave me a new name and it made me feel close to him, I like to think that God has given me a nickname too. As it says in Isaiah 56:5, it's a name better than sons and daughters. This name is an everlasting name; a name I will have as I live with Him forever.

I know one of the names He gives to you and me: His. We are His and I am so thankful we are!

LIVING CHERISHED

If you could choose a nickname God would give to you, what would it be? Why did you choose that nickname?

....

....

....

TALKING WITH GOD

God, thank You for loving me so deeply that You give me a name that is even better than "daughter." In Jesus' name, amen.

DAY 34

I WANT TO BE LIKED

Lynn

*Then you will experience for yourselves
the truth, and the truth will free you.*
JOHN 8:32 MSG

Opening my little gold diary, the first thing I see is an aster-isk with this note: *means when a boy started liking or quit liking me.* Being liked was so important to me, I had to make a note of it in my diary!

Seeing this handwritten message says a lot to me about the girl I was. I began to believe that if I was liked, I was valuable and cherished. If I wasn't liked, something was wrong with me.

I couldn't have been more wrong, but it would take me many, many years before I knew that.

In John 8, Jesus is talking to some people who were wondering exactly who He was. Jesus knew who He was: He was the perfect Son of God who had come into the world to die for our sins. He was the only One who could make it possible for us to have a relationship with God. Jesus told these people what would happen if they chose to believe the truth of who He was: "Then you will experience for yourselves the truth, and the truth will free you" (v. 32).

Free them from what?

One of the meanings of the word "free" is "unattached." These people had attached their worth and value to the wrong thing. They thought God would approve of them if they worked hard to be perfect. That wasn't true!

I was also attached to the wrong thing as a child. Having someone like me didn't mean I was cherished. I was *already* cherished because God loved me and I was His. Once I understood His love better, I didn't work as hard to make people like me. It's amazing what God's love can do!

LIVING CHERISHED

Take a moment to think about what makes you feel cherished. Like me, do you attach feeling loved to the wrong things? What are some Bible verses you can use to remind yourself that your worth and value are in God's great love for you?

....

....

....

TALKING TO GOD

Jesus, thank You for showing us the truth—the only way we can have a relationship with God is through You. I pray that this truth will help me realize I do not have to work to make people, or You, like me. You already and always love me. In Jesus' name, amen.

WHAT IF I GET LOST?

Lynn

"If a man has a hundred sheep and one of them wanders away, what will he do? Won't he leave the ninety-nine others on the hills and go out to search for the one that is lost?"

MATTHEW 18:12 NLT

My chest felt like the big drum from music class was banging inside. The store we were shopping in suddenly felt gigantic and scary as I realized I was separated from Mom. I had no idea where she was (or where I was for that matter). Panicking, I didn't care who saw me bawling—I just needed my mom! Then a kind woman stopped her shopping and led me to customer service. My mom's name was called over the loudspeaker, and soon her distraught face came around the corner. She had been searching for me. Now, hand-in-hand, we could wipe our tears and go home.

Have you ever been lost in a store, an airport, on a hike, or someplace worse?

Being lost makes us feel unprotected and helpless. We long for someone to come and find us.

In Matthew 18:12 (NIV), Jesus describes how He comes for us: "If a man owns a hundred sheep, and one of them wanders away, will he not leave the ninety-nine on the hills and go to look for the one that wandered off?" Jesus isn't talking about literally going into the woods or a park to find us. Instead, He is referring to when we have lost our way in life. When our family is falling apart, our friends no longer want to be friends, or we have to change schools we can feel lost. When things are not the way they used to be, we can feel sad or mad. We wonder if we'll ever be happy again.

Jesus tells us that even when we feel we've lost our way, He comes for us. He finds us right where we are, whether we chose to wander away or whether we feel others have left us. He does whatever it takes to come for us and show us His love.

LIVING CHERISHED

If you've ever gotten lost, describe how you felt when you were lost and then how you felt when you were found. Do you think the same thing can happen in our relationship with God?

....

....

....

TALKING WITH GOD

Jesus, I don't want to wander from You. If I lose my way at any time, I know You won't be mad at me, but will come for me. In Jesus' name, amen.

HE LEADS ME

Lynn

The Lord is my shepherd; I have all that I
need. He lets me rest in green meadows; he
leads me beside peaceful streams. He renews
my strength. He guides me along right paths,
bringing honor to his name.

PSALM 23:1–3 NLT

*S*hould I stay at this school or go to that one?

That's a big decision! And when I was only 11 years old,
it was a decision my parents said I could make on my own.

If I stayed at one school, I could keep all the friends I had
had for many years. It was the school my best friend and
neighbor went to. If I chose the other school, I could have
new opportunities that I never had before. *What was the right
decision?*

There are times in our lives when we have to make choices:
good, hard, or even fun choices. Sometimes we don't know
which way to go. It is during these times that I find God's
words to us so comforting. He tells us He is our shepherd; our
guide. The place that He will guide me to is along right paths
that are good for me and also give Him honor.

Sometimes it means that what I need to do is slow down,
not make a decision so quickly, and wait for Him to give me
what I need. Then, when I find the answer through His Word,
a wise counselor, or I sense that one way is the right way, I can
trust that my Shepherd is giving me exactly what I need.

LIVING CHERISHED

What is the job of a shepherd, and why would the Lord call Himself that? Use the internet or ask a grown-up to help you with your answer.

....

....

....

TALKING WITH GOD

Lord, thank You that because of Your great love for me, You will guide me in every area of my life. In Jesus' name, amen.

RESTING YOUR MIND

MICHELLE

Even though I walk through the darkest valley,
I will fear no evil, for you are with me; your rod
and your staff, they comfort me.

PSALM 23:4 NIV

I t's all just too much."

Have you ever said that? I have, especially when I feel overwhelmed. But you know what? Kids can get stressed out too. They have to get up early, do homework, remember to bring things to school, and wear their tennis shoes on PE days. Add in tests, chores, fearful thoughts, and after-school activities such as football, dance, soccer, cheer, and church . . . well, it can equal feeling sad, irritable, and like you're running on empty.

We need time to refuel and restore ourselves. Some kids find it through distractions like YouTube, video games, and TV. But these activities still require our eyes, brains, and often our hands to be engaged.

You were created for *rest*. You not only need a decent night's sleep to fuel your body with energy and your mind with focus, but you need opportunities to chill out, just breathe, use your imagination, and rest your body and mind.

Another way to find restoration is to connect with God. He can be the "lifter of your head," which means He can encourage you with positive thoughts. He can also restore your soul. I remember when I was young it was hard for me to sit still.

In my work as a counselor helping stressed-out families, I've learned how stillness can make a difference in mind and body. I now love just sitting outside sometimes doing nothing, walking the dog by myself, or stretching my body in bed. All of these things allow me to relax, and I find that God truly uses these things to provide the mindset and energy needed for the busy lives we lead.

He will do the same for you. At first, slowing down like this will feel weird. It's normal for your mind to wander while you're trying this new thing. But try taking time to focus on your breathing and enjoy the moment you are in, instead of worrying about what has already happened or all that you have to do.

LIVING CHERISHED

Set a timer for five minutes and go outside by yourself. Look at the sky. Breathe in, count to three, and breathe out, counting to three. On the lines below, write down what you noticed during your five minutes of stillness—sounds, smells, sights, or thoughts that popped into your head.

....

....

....

TALKING WITH GOD

Father, thanks for modeling rest for us and encouraging us to set aside time to do the same so our brains and bodies don't burn out. Help me to remember that You can restore the energy and positivity I need during busy times when it's so easy to become stressed out. In Jesus' name, amen.

UNAFRAID OF UNCOMFORTABLE

Lynn

At that very time Jesus cured many who had diseases, sicknesses and evil spirits, and gave sight to many who were blind.

LUKE 7:21 NIV

When my dad was sick, I dreaded going to the hospital. I loved my dad, but being in a place full of sick people made me uncomfortable. I know I'm not the only one. Sometimes people struggle with going to the hospital because it brings back their own bad memories. Sickness and disease . . . well, it's just not something we're drawn to. So, often, we avoid being around those who are not well.

When Jesus was on the earth, He didn't avoid people who made Him uncomfortable. He loved people; *all* people. Jesus was unafraid to hug the hurting and pull close the sick. He did whatever it took for those people to be whole again.

There was nothing that was too much for Jesus. Luke 7:22 tells us that when close to Jesus the blind receive sight, those who couldn't walk did, and those with oozing skin sores were healed. Yes, Jesus was unafraid to give them His touch! The deaf were healed, the dead were raised to life, and the good news of His forgiveness and unconditional love were proclaimed to the poor. No one was left out.

Jesus spoke of His love for us, but even greater than that, Jesus *showed* His love for us.

You and I can be confident that no matter what condition or situation we may find ourselves in, Jesus reaches out to us, drawing us in. He whispers to us, "Come close. I am here for you."

LIVING CHERISHED

Have you ever felt, or do you ever feel, that there are reasons Jesus wouldn't want you close to Him? What are they?

....

....

....

Now read out loud the list below of those Jesus drew close. Remember, none of the reasons you wrote down above will stop His love for you—He is pulling you close as well!

> ". . . The blind receive sight, the lame walk, those who have leprosy are cleansed, the deaf hear, the dead are raised, and the good news is proclaimed to the poor."
>
> LUKE 7:22B

TALKING WITH GOD

Lord, thank You that there is never any reason You would not want me close to You. Help me respond to You pulling me in to receive the perfect love You have for me today. In Jesus' name, amen.

DAY 39

SAFE AT NIGHT

MICHELLE

*In peace I will lie down and sleep, for you alone,
LORD, make me dwell in safety.*
PSALM 4:8 NIV

"Mom, can I sleep in your bed with you?" I turned over to see my son standing in the doorway to my room. Glancing at the clock, I saw it was about one in the morning.

"I had a really bad dream. You and Daddy both died and I couldn't find Sissy," he said.

Nighttime gives our brains a chance to come up with crazy ideas. And when we wake up alone and in the dark, we're often scared almost out of our minds. But we aren't truly alone.

We can actually train our minds to know and believe we are safe and sleep in peace because God promises to be with us always and keep us safe. If you struggle with bedtime thoughts, it's a great idea to get a sleep journal and write them down or draw out the scary things in your head. It will help if you get it out of your mind and onto paper where you are bigger and things look smaller.

I think that is what David did when he wrote, "In peace I will lie down and sleep, for you alone, LORD, make me dwell in safety" (Psalm 4:8).

You can also pray and remind yourself that God is watching over you, and find comfort that the creator of the universe is an awesome protector. He wants to help us fight the fear that can invade our minds and make our bodies so tense that our stomachs hurt.

In our counseling offices, we read books for kids about conquering bedtime worries that help them choose phrases they can say out loud when they're scared. My son likes to say, "Get away devil. Stop making me scared." Some kids choose "even though" statements such as "Even though I may feel scared, I know I am safe." Others make huge posters reminding themselves they can shrink their fears by looking at pictures that make them smile and have courage.

I am confident that if you practice resting in God's safety, as bedtime comes you will enjoy better rest and more peaceful nights.

LIVING CHERISHED

Decide on a phrase you will use if you feel scared at night and write it down below. Practice saying it so it will come naturally to you when you are scared.

....

....

....

TALKING WITH GOD

God, thank You for being with me at night and watching over me. Help me to see that You are the giant who moves mountains so You can shrink my fears. Thank You for giving me peace when I ask You for it. In Jesus' name, amen.

YOU'RE NOT DEFINED BY YOUR MISTAKES

LYNN

And if he finds it, I tell you the truth, he will rejoice over it more than over the ninety-nine that didn't wander away!

MATTHEW 18:13 NLT

We were the loud ones, and our teacher was tired of it. Worn out with trying to teach us to be quiet, my friends and I were put on restriction during lunch, meaning we would eat lunch each day with only our teacher.

While I knew our teacher was trying to teach us to have self-control, this wasn't the message my friend Julie got. She struggled with thoughts that each mistake she made meant *she* was a mistake. "Bad behavior equals a bad person," her mind told her. These untruths pushed Julie further and further away from Jesus. If the teacher believed she was bad, then maybe Jesus did too. So, she began to wander from Him because she didn't understand how great His love was for her.

In Matthew 18, Jesus is teaching using a story that my Bible calls "The Parable of the Lost Sheep." In it, Jesus says that if one of the shepherd's sheep intentionally leaves, the shepherd goes after the sheep. In this story we need to understand that Jesus is actually saying that the Father is the shepherd and we are the sheep. So you know what sticks out to me? Jesus didn't say if we (the sheep) get lost or accidentally go the wrong way, but instead says "wander way." So even if we go astray on purpose, the Shepherd comes after us. God leaves everything to come and find us, bringing us back to Him. When He finds us, He is joyful! He's so glad we are finally home. This is how much we are cherished by Him!

This story catches me by surprise because I would have thought like Julie—that God would punish us for going off the right path. But He does the opposite. Because of His great love for us, He rejoices because we are back with Him once again.

LIVING CHERISHED

Think of a time when you misbehaved on purpose or made an accidental mistake. Did you feel like *you* were bad, or did you understand that it was *your actions* that were bad? What does God say about who you are as a person?

....

....

....

TALKING WITH GOD

God, Your love for me blows me away. It is deeper than I thought. Please help me keep understanding more and more about how great Your love is for me. In Jesus' name, amen.

YOU ARE WORTHY

Lynn

I am no longer worthy to be called your son;
make me like one of your hired servants.
LUKE 15:19 NIV

It's not worth it," I thought. A long time ago, I kept trying to be friends with a certain person but just when things got better, they got bad again. It was like we couldn't stay out of drama. There was a lot of, "You said this," and, "Well, you did that." I was finally at the end of trying. I had decided the friendship was no longer *worth* the fight.

Worth it. It's how we decide who makes the cut; who we get to know, be friends with, or love. Sometimes we make the choice that no matter how hard it is, the relationship **is** worth the work.

What does "worth" mean, anyway?

The word "worth" means "Having great value or being deserving." We decide, even if we are not aware of it, whether someone is of great value to us or deserving of our friendship and love.

In Luke 15, Jesus tells a story of a son who is extremely disrespectful and unloving toward his father. He runs away from home, wasting everything his father gave him. When the son becomes broke and is starving, he decides to go back home. On his way, he plans what he is going to say when he sees his father: "I am no longer worthy to be called your son; make me like one of your hired servants" (v. 19).

When the father sees his son, still a long way off, the father's pure love takes over his heart. ". . . he ran to his son, threw his arms around him and kissed him" (v. 20b).

Here's what the son missed—he said he was "no longer worthy to be called" his son. The son's words show us that he was confused. He thought his *actions* made him deserving of great value. But what truly made the son of great value was the fact that he was greatly loved! The father makes this clear by running toward the son before the son even says a word.

The same is true for you. You are worthy. You are of great value not because of what you do or don't do. You're not valuable because you get it all right or always do what is right. You are worthy and of great value because, like the son, you are wildly loved by the Father!

LIVING CHERISHED

How have you felt in the past about God's love? Describe it the best you can. Is that picture beginning to change as we read the truth in His Word? If so, how?

....

....

....

TALKING WITH GOD

Father, thank You that my worth has nothing to do with what I do and everything to do with who You are . . . my perfect, loving Father. In Jesus' name, amen.

RUNNING TO ME

Lynn

So he returned home to his father. And while he was still a long way off, his father saw him coming. Filled with love and compassion, he ran to his son, embraced him, and kissed him.

LUKE 15:20 NLT

Have you ever felt like running away from home? I remember one day being so upset, I packed my backpack, hopped on my bike, and headed out. I don't remember much more than that . . . except I didn't get far and I couldn't wait to get home once I headed back that way.

In "The Parable of the Lost Son" in Luke 15, the son rejected his father; rejected his whole family. Only, unlike me, he was old enough to leave home and stay gone for a long time. His actions would have been very hurtful and upsetting to his family.

Some of us have also had a brother or sister, or even a parent, leave us. Maybe you know what it feels like to have your love for someone pushed away.

One reason I love this story so much is because it shows how Jesus understands our feelings of rejection. He created us, then came to earth and died for us . . . and yet, some of us reject His love.

I find comfort knowing that Jesus understands when I feel rejected because He feels rejected too. I'm grateful that on the days I run from His love by trying to do everything on my own and in my own way, He waits for me to return to Him. And when I do, He's right there, running to me, His arms open wide.

LIVING CHERISHED

Who or what has made you feel rejected? Ask Jesus to heal that hurt with His love that we are learning so much about. What's your favorite way to remember that God chooses you to be His own?

....
....
....

TALKING WITH GOD

Dear God, I am so grateful that Your love for me is not based on what I do or don't do but is instead based on who You are as my loving, heavenly Father. In Jesus' name, amen.

MORE THAN I DESERVE

LYNN

*But the father said to his servants, "Quick!
Bring the best robe and put it on him. Put a
ring on his finger and sandals on his feet."*

LUKE 15:22 NIV

Have you ever made up an apology or an excuse in your mind, to give to your parents as soon as they walked in the door? "Mom, I didn't mean to break your lamp." "Dad, I didn't get the dog poop scooped because . . ."

In the story Jesus told called "The Parable of the Lost Son" in Luke 15, the son finally comes home after running away and making a big mess of his life. After working for a pig farmer for food, he must have looked awful as he made his way back home. That's about the time the father comes running toward him and the son begins to make the speech he worked on during his walk.

Just as the son opens his mouth to apologize for all the ways he messed up, the father interrupts him, calling to those working for him, "Quick! Bring the best robe and put it on him. Put a ring on his finger and sandals on his feet" (v. 22).

See, the father doesn't just *tell* his child that he is loved and cherished. He *shows* him by giving him what he needs. In fact, the father doesn't just give his child what he needs, he is very generous and provides beyond his needs. He gives his child the best of what he has!

God shows you how much you are loved each and every day as well. When the sun comes up every day, the Father shows His faithful love for you. The fact that you have breath, food, and a place to sleep shows that your Father provides for you because He cherishes you.

LIVING CHERISHED

Think of the things in your life that you don't have to worry about; things that are signs that you are loved and taken care of. List them here.

....

....

....

TALKING WITH GOD

Thank You, Father God, that You are eager to give me Your best; Your perfect, unconditional love shooting right at this heart of mine that You made. In Jesus' name, amen.

DAY 44

SWEET FRIENDSHIPS

MICHELLE

Perfume and incense bring joy to the heart, and the pleasantness of a friend springs from their heartfelt advice.

PROVERBS 27:9 NIV

Friends are the best! My daughter and her friends sometimes act so crazy in the car, but all the singing and laughing tells me they're really happy. Happiness is contagious. Happy friends can make a hard day so much better.

Do you want more happy friends?

Well, the first step you can take toward having them is to be a happy friend. What are you grateful for? I believe happiness is a state of mind that comes not from our circumstances, but by the thoughts we choose to think as we wake up in the morning, get in our car, walk in the hallways, come home from a long day, and get ready for bed.

Once we become happier people, others are attracted to our joy. It's also a great idea to surround ourselves with others who are making the same types of choices. Look around your school, team, and church. Choose a few people who seem to be happy most of the time. (I've never met anyone who's *always* happy.) You will need a few because some already have all the friends they need for the time being or the two of you might not click well.

Next, try to be around them more often. Maybe sit with them at lunch or ask if you can join in on their fun during free time. Friendships begin in small steps. After some time in school together, talk to your mom about inviting them over after school or on the weekends. Time together talking and making memories is how friendship begins.

LIVING CHERISHED

If you already have a great friend who brings joy to your life, give thanks for them. If you are struggling with friendships or surrounding yourself with happy people, start today by choosing to be a happier person yourself. As you start to feel better inside, seek out happy people around you and spend more time with them. Who are some happy people in your life you can list right now?

....

....

....

TALKING TO GOD

Father, I want to be surrounded by people who bring joy to my life. Help me be one of those joyful people and spend my time around others who choose to smile and look at life with an attitude of gratitude. In Jesus' name, amen.

HOW TO BE HAPPY

Lynn

Happy are those who hear the joyful call to worship, for they will walk in the light of your presence, Lord.

PSALM 89:15 NLT

Do you think it's possible to *learn* to be happy?

I love to be happy. It's a silly thing to say, I know. But doesn't everyone love to be happy?

Happy isn't like a light switch we can just turn on when we want to. But there's something we can do to help our hearts to be happy!

In Psalm 89, the writer says those who are happy are those who worship the Lord. Why would that be? I, for one, don't always feel like worshiping God . . . *especially* if I am having a bad day or things aren't going the way I would like them to.

The writer goes on to tell us why they are happy. ". . . for they will walk in the light of your presence, Lord" (v. 15).

When we worship the Lord, He lifts up our heart. He gives us His joy and peace. He takes away our fears.

How do you worship Him? You can worship Him through talking with Him, singing to Him, and reading His Word. You can paint Him a picture, write Him a song, run like the wind as you think of His greatness. You can get out in nature and enjoy the beauty of all He has made. You could create a vase out of clay, plant a flower and think on His creativity. You could serve an elderly neighbor and share His love with another.

There are countless ways that we can worship Him. When we do, we will experience His presence and it will make us happy.

LIVING CHERISHED

In the space below, list some ways you can worship God and bring him praise. For example, you could sing Him a song, run as fast as you can while thanking him for the gift of your health, draw Him a picture, write Him a story, make up a dance for Him, or whatever else you want to do that simply says, "You are amazing, God!"

....

....

....

TALKING WITH GOD

God, You make me happy. Your greatness, Your love, and Your faithfulness are good. I love You, God. In Jesus' name, amen.

STRONG ENOUGH

MICHELLE

*The LORD is my strength and my shield; my
heart trusts in him, and he helps me. My heart
leaps for joy, and with my song I praise him.*

PSALM 28:7 NIV

All through school I hated push-ups, chin-ups, and pull-ups. To be honest, my upper body is pretty weak. I have never met a person without some type of weakness. Some kids have learning disabilities, some aren't great at sports, and others feel they can't draw or sing very well. Lots of people struggle with speaking in front of the class.

Being imperfect is part of our human experience. And I believe the sooner we accept our weaknesses, the easier our lives become. I also know that there is good news for all of us! God can be our strength when we are weak. We can tap into God's supernatural strength every day to do the hard things we don't like—even pull-ups.

So, what's hard for you? God understands and wants to help! Talk to him today and ask Him to help you tap into His amazing strength. He may lead you to work daily at becoming stronger, reading better, or learning that skill that seems too hard.

Sometimes when God works in us, He makes us better by building what's called "perseverance" which just means our ability to keep doing something hard. Just remember: if you've turned to Him and worked hard, whatever happens is good enough! Even if it's only one push-up, a C for a grade, or you give your presentation in front of your class with butterflies in your stomach anyway.

LIVING CHERISHED

Pick a weakness that often bothers you and talk to God about it. Ask Him to help you, and then join with Him in creating a plan to work hard at getting better. What steps can you and God take together? List them below.

....

....

....

TALKING WITH GOD

Father, I hate that I stink at _____. Help me to trust in You to show Your strength in me. Thank You for helping me with my weaknesses. In Jesus' name, amen.

YOU MADE ME THIS WAY

LYNN

No, don't say that. Who are you, a mere human being, to argue with God? Should the thing that was created say to the one who created it, "Why have you made me like this?"

ROMANS 9:20 NLT

As we walked into the painting studio, my mother and I could feel the excitement from other mothers and daughters who were about to try something new. My mom and I found our spot, ready to begin.

Following the instructions of the teacher, there was chatter and laughter, as each painter created the background for their masterpiece. *I can do that!* I thought, studying the example the instructor held up. Soon, the easy part ended. Then it was time to fill in the details of the painting.

The project turned out to be harder than I thought, and I laughed with Mom about how my painting was *not* a re-creation of our teacher's. For the young girl near me though, it was no joke. Frustration took over. Tears hung on her lower lashes as she tried to keep it together.

Suddenly, grabbing her paintbrush, her tears overflowed. She scrubbed her canvas, her brush loaded with black paint, trying her best to ruin her creation.

Her painting was not like the model and she couldn't take the disappointment in herself. Running from her failure, she bolted from the room. She wanted her painting to look just like those around her. She didn't see *her own unique masterpiece*.

Sometimes we can do the same as we look in the mirror. We hope to see one thing, but painfully feel we see something different. Yet our Creator says to us, "No, don't say that. Who are you, a mere human being, to argue with God? Should the thing that was created say to the one who created it, 'Why have you made me like this?'" (Romans 9:20).

God made us exactly the way we are because this is how He defines beautiful. And as our Creator, His definition is right! We need to listen to His words about who we are, blocking voices that say differently, even when that voice is our own. God can help us do that!

LIVING CHERISHED

In the space below, jot down some ideas of verses that tell you how God sees you. You can find some examples in the Meditation Matters section on page 79. Write these verses out on sticky notes or cards so you can put them on a mirror you look at daily and read them each time you pass by.

....

....

....

TALKING WITH GOD

Lord, thank You for making me the way You did. Help me to see myself as You see me. In Jesus' name, amen.

FIGHTING FOR ME

LYNN

"The second most important commandment says: 'Love others as much as you love yourself.' No other commandment is more important than these."

MARK 12:31 CEV

There is nothing quite like a fight with a friend to make a girl feel rotten. At least that's often the direction my feelings want to go when hurtful words are hurled my way.

When emotions get hot, all too often our first reaction is to not remember how God sees us and that we are treasured by Him. Instead, we can take those words and replay them over and over again in our minds. And the more they spin around in our minds, the more we believe that what the person said was in fact true.

Can I give you a challenge?

When a fight with a friend begins brewing, instead of fighting *with* her, fight *for* you.

Fight for me?

Yes! See, it is in the middle of these potentially damaging outbursts that people say words that often they don't mean, but even more importantly, they say words that are simply not true.

So when you hear words like, "You *always* . . ." or "You *never* . . .", it's a sign that it's time for you to walk away and not fight with her, but fight for you.

110

Fight to protect your heart, the one God lovingly created and cherishes. Avoid the attack; shut down the app. Love back the one that God loves so much . . . *you!*

When you walk away from a fight, not only are you loving yourself by stepping away or shutting social media down, but you are loving your friend too. You are choosing to stop the conversation before you have the opportunity to turn around and hurt her as well. In Mark 12:31, Jesus tells us, "The second most important commandment says: 'Love others as much as you love yourself.' No other commandment is more important than these." Love others *as much as* you love yourself. So, if you are going to love the way Jesus loves, it begins with loving yourself, and loving yourself well.

LIVING CHERISHED

Think about the last fight you had with a friend. How could you have backed out of the conversation before you or your friend got hurt? What will you do next time it seems like a conversation is heading toward an argument?

....

....

....

TALKING WITH GOD

God, sometimes I'm scared that hurtful comments might be hurled at me, so I throw the first punch. Give me the courage to be the one who stops the fight before it even begins. In Jesus' name, amen.

JESUS GETS IT

LYNN

> The soldiers took Jesus into the palace (called Praetorium) and called together the entire brigade. They dressed him up in purple and put a crown plaited from a thorn bush on his head. Then they began their mockery: "Bravo, King of the Jews!" They banged on his head with a club, spit on him, and knelt down in mock worship. After they had had their fun, they took off the purple cape and put his own clothes back on him. Then they marched out to nail him to the cross.
>
> MARK 15:16–20 MSG

Being made fun of—wow, can it ever hurt! I've been made fun of for many things, like my body and my laugh, but mostly for being "so good." I've always had a tender conscience, not wanting to do what my parents or God would disapprove of. I simply wanted to do what was right. Often, that didn't go over well and I was on the receiving end of teasing.

While the teasing hurt my feelings, what hurt most of all was feeling alone. Sometimes it felt like I was the only person who wanted to do what was right. I didn't like being home alone because my friends were doing something I wasn't comfortable with. But at the same time, I wanted to please God more than I wanted to feel accepted by my friends.

Jesus really gets what it's like to be teased and made fun of. In Mark 15, before Jesus died on the cross, He experienced cruel teasing. They made fun of Him for saying He was the Son of God. The truth was that Jesus *was* the Son of God. That's what made Him so great . . . and exactly what they didn't see.

That thing they make fun of you for? It's most likely the very thing that makes you great! In fact, it is probably your very own superpower.

Remember that desire I had to please God? It's exactly what helped me make a lot of good and right choices over the years. God helped me find peace about the very thing I was pestered about.

Next time you feel alone when you are mocked or made fun of, remember Jesus gets you. Ask Him to help you see this as your superpower and a reminder that you are loved by Him.

LIVING CHERISHED

Is there something that you get teased for? Something about your body or the way you act? Ask God how you can see this as something good—maybe even your very own superpower!

....

....

....

TALKING WITH GOD

God, I know You made me, and You made me unique. I need Your help to see the parts of me that others pick on as things that can be good. Give me eyes to see myself the way You see me. In Jesus' name, amen.

GOOD THINGS

MICHELLE

Sovereign LORD, you are God! Your covenant is trustworthy, and you have promised these good things to your servant.

2 SAMUEL 7:28 NIV

"Mom, did you get the email yet?" I heard this phrase over and over as my daughter anxiously awaited audition results. Yesterday, it finally came and she made it! I can't tell you as parents how excited my husband and I were for her. We smiled and celebrated as the talents we truly believe were created in her by God were not only recognized, but also would be further developed.

God doesn't just want to meet you during the hard times. He wants to be included in the good ones as well. God has promised good things for your life. I want you to know this in your head and believe it in your heart. I want you to try hard, scary things so you can fully experience His goodness as you head toward becoming an adult. You won't always get selected but you'll never be considered if you don't try.

And if you don't make it the first time? You may have to do some hard work and try more than once, and that's okay! I watched my daughter and her friends work hard for this audition. They practiced for hours together and then even more on their own. She took additional lessons to prepare and received some tough feedback, but it made her better.

My prayer for you today is that you will trust God's promises for good in your life and do the hard work so you can experience the joy that comes from chasing after the dreams He's placed in your heart.

LIVING CHERISHED

Make a list of some really good things that have happened in your life since you were born. Take a moment to celebrate these moments, placing God in the picture as you think about them.

....

....

....

TALKING WITH GOD

God, I celebrate that You have promised good things in my life. Help me to believe this even when I can't see them. Help me seek them knowing that You are there beside me every step of the way. In Jesus' name, amen.

GOD UNDERSTANDS ME

LYNN

See what great love the Father has lavished on us, that we should be called children of God! And that is what we are! The reason the world does not know us is that it did not know him.

1 JOHN 3:1 NIV

It didn't matter how many times I tried to explain myself, my friend just couldn't get how I felt. She couldn't, or *wouldn't*, understand me. I wasn't sure which it was.

Whether it's with a coach, a teacher, or even your best friend, there will be times when people misunderstand us. I know for me these moments leave me frustrated and often feeling lonely. *Doesn't anyone get me?*

We want to be known; to feel like someone understands the things that make us the way we are.

I find so much comfort in knowing that the One who made me understands me. He carefully created my mind, my personality, and all the things that make me unique! He never finds me strange or weird. He sees the dance parties I have alone in my bathroom. He knows what I dream when I am all alone. He loves the things that make me unique, and He treasures them!

In fact, His love for us is so great, the Bible uses the word "lavish" to describe it. This love is given to us in such great amounts that it's without limit.

This relationship you have with God has the potential to be so deep, so beautiful, and so perfect, it doesn't make sense to some people. They have a hard time thinking it can be real or that it makes a difference. In fact, they might even fight against it.

While we keep on sharing so that they, too, can know this life-changing truth for themselves, we also must keep in mind that sometimes people won't get you because they don't understand God. While that hurts, it's true that I don't have to be understood by all to be understood by God. The fact that you are loved and understood by Him is what truly matters.

LIVING CHERISHED

You don't have to be understood by all to be understood by God. Practice saying to yourself, "God loves me and God gets me." What feelings come to you as you repeat this phrase? Write them down now.

....

....

....

TALKING WITH GOD

God, I am so glad You get me. You understand me. Help me remember this truth on days when I feel so alone. In Jesus' name, amen.

ALL THE COMPARING

LYNN

*Through him all things were made; without
him nothing was made that has been made.*
JOHN 1:3 NIV

As I read through my diary, I see entries filled with things I
did: piano concerts, music performances, and plays. Each
entry is usually followed up with how I did at these performances and all too often the words I used to describe myself
weren't very kind. *Not great. Didn't do well. Should have done better.*

I would guess that what I was comparing myself to was
the performances of others; the perfect piece played by the
student in front of me. The solo by the singer who sounded
like an angel. The lines spoken without hesitation through the
entire play. The standard was other people.

I wish I could go back and tell my younger self: *You are not
other people. You are you; created by a perfect God just the way He
saw fit. You don't have to perform. You can be free to not worry about
what others think. You don't have to be like them, and you can enjoy
being you.*

Easier said than done, right? I know this truth, but even
now, I have to remind myself what God said—He made me the
way He made me, and that's a very good thing!

"Through him all things were made; without him nothing
was made that has been made." John 1:3 says this. But why
does this even matter? Since God is perfect, all He creates is
beautiful, lovely, and good. That includes *you!*

Our culture runs off making us unhappy with ourselves. Money is made by creating discontentment. When I was growing up, curly hair was so in! We actually permed our hair to get it super curly when I was growing up! Now it's a negative thing called "frizzy," so we have to fix it. There were no hair straightening products in the past. Can you see the plot to get us to pay to get rid of our problems? Problems that culture created to get us to spend money.

Comparison is always a losing game. When we catch ourselves comparing ourselves to others, we must remember again: God is perfect, all He creates is beautiful, lovely, and good. That includes you!

LIVING CHERISHED

Do you find yourself getting stuck in thought patterns of comparing yourself to others? What are some thoughts you can think, Bible verses you can reflect on, or promises from God you can fill your mind with instead?

....

....

....

TALKING WITH GOD

God, it's hard to remember that each one of us is different, and that different is good. Help me to spot when the world around me is trying to make me unhappy with the way You made me. In Jesus' name, amen.

BE KIND TO YOURSELF

LYNN

So God created human beings in his own image.
In the image of God he created them; male and
female he created them . . . Then God looked over
all he had made, and he saw that it was very good!
GENESIS 1:27, 31A NLT

*I*just want to look like everyone else, I thought, *especially like those* *girls on TV.*

It didn't take long for me to notice that as our bodies started changing, they weren't all changing at the same time or in the same way. Some girls were so much taller than me; others were staying the same height as the grade before. Some of us started gaining weight, in all different places, while others were teased for being what others thought was "too" skinny.

One thing we all had in common; we were uncertain about what this time in our lives—this time of body change—was supposed to look like. Was what the kids at school were saying really true? Was there a "perfect" body and a "weird" body?

As I become more mature, I'm learning there is one source that we can *always* count on for telling us the truth: God's Word.

Genesis 1:27 and 31a says, "So God created human beings in his own image. In the image of God he created them; male and female he created them . . . Then God looked over all he had made, and he saw that it was very good!"

Later, in Psalm 18:30 (NIV), it says, "As for God, his way is perfect . . ."

So this perfect God, in the very beginning, created people. Humans were His idea; and a really good one too! You and I were created by God, the One whose way is always perfect. And while there are times when we look at His creation of us and wonder what's going on, the one thing we don't need to doubt is whether He's doing a good job. He knows exactly what He is doing in you. What we need to focus on is being kind to ourselves, treasuring ourselves, just as He treasures us.

LIVING CHERISHED

What part of your body do you like the most? Is it your eyes that see God's goodness all around you? Your smile that reflects the warmth of God's love to others? Your arms that reach out to hug someone who needs comfort? Your feet that carry you to new ways to serve? When you find yourself focusing on what you don't like about your body, practice pulling your mind back to all of the ways God has created you beautifully.

TALKING WITH GOD

God, it helps to remember that You know exactly what You are doing. Please help me learn to trust that You created me just the way You wanted me to be! In Jesus' name, amen.

IT'S POSSIBLE WITH GOD

MICHELLE

I can do all this through him who gives me strength.

PHILIPPIANS 4:13 NIV

Have you ever been asked to do something that seemed impossible? For me, writing lots of words in a book seemed that way. I like to talk more than I like to write. And, I have a sister who is just the opposite! Writing words comes easy to her, but she doesn't like speaking on the radio when she doesn't have a script.

Our minds can sometimes lie to us. They may tell us we can't do something we've never done before or failed the one time we tried. In the Bible it says that all things are possible with God. I love that idea, especially when my mind is stuck in negative thoughts.

We have to remind our minds not to get stuck in negative thoughts, so we can grow and do impossible things with God as our helper. It's hard work but when we do this daily, we become more confident. That confidence energizes us to take on what seems impossible to us and do it better.

Maybe for you, that's a big test at school. In Texas, our students have to pass one in certain grades or they have to go to summer school. Important tests can create a lot of pressure. Maybe passing seems impossible. It might feel like you have to do difficult things by yourself, but God will be there right beside you through the hard things you face that seem impossible.

LIVING CHERISHED

In the space below, write a short prayer you can use when you need to take a deep breath and remember to depend on God, through whom all things are possible. Bookmark this page so you can come back to your prayer whenever you need it!

....

....

....

TALKING WITH GOD

God, thank You that with You all things can be possible for me. Help me to reprogram my stinkin' thinkin' that tells me "I can't do it." I am learning that nothing is impossible with You. In Jesus' name, amen.

DAY 55

A CROWN FOR KEEPS

Lynn

Let all that I am praise the LORD; may I never forget the good things he does for me. He forgives all my sins and heals all my diseases. He redeems me from death and crowns me with love and tender mercies.

PSALM 103:2–4 NLT

Have you ever saved a picture of a hairstyle you wanted to copy? A cool braid to try or some fancy twisty thing?

When I was 5, my sister who was 15 years older than me got married and I was her flower girl. Well, I had that picture of exactly the way I wanted to wear my hair. Forget the fact that I was 5 and wanted to look like my sister who was 20. I asked my sister, a hairdresser, to cut my hair just like hers. She said no, but I wasn't going to let that stop me!

So, I cut it myself. Let's just say it didn't go well, and I gave myself crooked bangs! That same summer, I was in another wedding in which I wore a flower crown. (Maybe it was because my haircut was still a mess!)

Walking down the aisle, that ring of roses floated on my head. Eventually, the celebrations ended, and I took the flower crown and dress off in exchange for my summertime shorts.

I don't remember much about either of those days. What I do remember is the smile on my face in the pictures, especially my grin with the crown on my head. I just loved to get dressed up and look pretty.

In Psalm 103:2–4, the writer is praising God by saying that He "crowns me with love and tender mercies."

Isn't that absolutely beautiful? You may or may not think a crown of roses is pretty, but everyone craves love. Our Creator crowns us with *love*.

This love is at the very center of who God is . . . God is love. His love is everlasting. His is not a love that's only given when loved in return. No, His love flows to us no matter what. Even if I quit loving Him, He won't quit loving me. He can't because love is the core of who God is. His crown of love for you will never come off.

LIVING CHERISHED

In the space below, draw yourself with a crown of beautiful flowers on your head, or write what your imaginary flower crown would look and smell like. Maybe you would choose a different material for your crown—if so, describe it!

TALKING WITH GOD

Jesus, the thought of You placing something of beauty on me is really special. Help me remember, especially on days when I feel unloved or unlovable, that You placed a crown of love on me that will never be removed. In Jesus' name, amen.

HIGH ABOVE IT ALL

LYNN

For his unfailing love toward those who fear him is as great as the height of the heavens above the earth.

PSALM 103:11 NLT

How do you feel about heights? Me? Well, if I ever was scared of heights, I surely got over it the day my daughter and I jumped out of a plane!

That day was like no other! I remember the jump making my stomach flip-flop and my head spin. Once we settled into floating though, I got a glimpse of what it would be like to be a bird. Looking up, the sky just went on and on and on, far past what I could see.

In Psalm 103:11, the writer says: "For his unfailing love toward those who fear him is as great as the height of the heavens above the earth." David describes God's love as "greater than the distance between heaven and earth!" (CEV) It goes on and on.

He says God's love is unfailing—it won't fall short of what we expect. His love is completely dependable and faithful. It's inexhaustible, meaning we can't burn it out! His love is endless.

That kind of love is almost impossible for us to understand. We've had people say they love us, but then they die, leave, or move away. The people who love us the most might get tired of us sometimes, grow impatient and need time alone and away from us. Yet this love is as great as the height of the heavens above the earth.

Even though I've been pretty high in the sky, I haven't come close to heaven. I think in the same way, we can try to understand how great His love for us is, but we won't even be close.

LIVING CHERISHED

Go outside and look up at the sky. Lay down in the grass if you can. Stay right there for a while, letting your eyes focus as far as they can see. What thoughts come to mind as you think about how God's love for you is higher than even your eyes can see? Write them out below.

....
....
....

TALKING WITH GOD

Wow, God! That's a whole lot of love. When I see the sky, I pray that it will remind me that even though I can see far, I'm not even close to knowing or understanding just how great Your love for me is! In Jesus' name, amen.

MOUTHWATERING WORDS

LYNN

When I discovered your words, I devoured them. They are my joy and my heart's delight, for I bear your name, O LORD God of Heaven's Armies.

JEREMIAH 15:16 NLT

Don't you just love reading a book you can't put down? When a story is that good, I get caught up in it, reading way into the night because I must see what happens next! My heart becomes happy as I look forward to an exciting ending!

In Jeremiah 15:16, Jeremiah says this is how he feels about God's amazing book, the Bible: "When I discovered your words, I devoured them."

Why would Jeremiah say God's Word is so delicious?

It is because of what Jeremiah says about God's words in the next sentence of Jeremiah 15:16 . . . "They are my joy and my heart's delight, for I bear your name." In this somewhat lonely world, where some days it feels like everything is falling apart and nothing is going well, God's Word fills our empty heart and heals our hurting places. It is here that He reminds us "I am called by your name" (ESV).

You are not a nobody; you are somebody's! You are God's own. His Word—His truth—fills our hearts with joy and happiness because we belong to Him.

When your heart's been hurt again by the one who calls

herself your best friend, you're feeling left out, or feel invisible, remember what is true and speak to your heart: I belong to God.

LIVING CHERISHED

Below, write how it feels to know that you are somebody's Somebody. Then, write "I'm His" on something you own to remind you of this truth every day. It could be on your notebook, a poster in your room, or even a T-shirt.

....

....

....

TALKING WITH GOD

Jesus, thank You that I belong to You. I am safe in this place because being Yours means that I am never alone—not today and not any day. In Jesus' name, amen.

NEVER ALONE

Lynn

I never sat in the company of revelers, never made merry with them; I sat alone because your hand was on me and you had filled me with indignation.

JEREMIAH 15:17 NIV

I laid on my bed, loud music playing, trying to keep myself from slipping down into self-pity. I had been left out . . . again. It hurt a lot, and I was tired of hurting.

I knew why they left me out. There were things I did, like obey my parents, that they thought were dumb. There were also things they did that I wouldn't do.

And so, here I was.

Alone again.

And yet, I was really not alone at all. Even though I was in my bedroom by myself, God was with me.

In Jeremiah 15, the prophet is really struggling. He was left out and felt that blow deeply. But even in this place, he says "I sat alone because your hand was on me." Jeremiah recognized God had something to do with why he sat alone. In fact, God was the *reason* he was alone; and it was a good reason.

As I look back on those sometimes lonely times I, too, can say, "I sat alone because your hand was on me." Whether it was because I said "no" to doing something I didn't feel was right or because God protected me from being in places where I shouldn't have been, it was actually good for me to be alone.

I know that being alone hurts sometimes. It takes a really mature girl to look at occasionally being alone as a good thing. I just want to reassure you, that God *always* has your best future at heart. You can trust Him, even when it hurts.

LIVING CHERISHED

Can you think of a time when you weren't included in something, but later realized it was a good thing? If not, try asking your parent or guardian if something like that ever happened to them. When we look back on these times and on our history with God, it can help us to trust Him when life hurts.

....

....

....

TALKING WITH GOD

God, I really don't like feeling alone. Remind me that when I sit alone, I am never really on my own. In Jesus' name, amen.

WATCHING OVER ME

LYNN

I lift up my eyes to the mountains—where does my help come from? My help comes from the LORD, the Maker of heaven and earth. He will not let your foot slip—he who watches over you will not slumber.

PSALM 121:1-3 NIV

When I was growing up, most of the time I felt behind. In each grade, I was one of the youngest in class because I had a summer birthday. Being the youngest meant I was often one of the smallest kids in my grade. Since my parents based many privileges on age, it meant I experienced some privileges later than other kids in my grade. With a birthday so close to the 4th of July, it also meant I often didn't get to have big birthday celebrations because most of the time people were on vacation. Sometimes, I felt like I was in the wrong place at the wrong time. I feared I was missing out on all of the best things.

Though I was sad, the Lord comforted me. He helped me get through those times of feeling left out of what was going on.

As we get older, sometimes we are able to look back and see things a different way.

So now as I look back, I really do see what I couldn't see then. I wasn't really missing out. During those times, God was working in me. He was preparing me so that I would have the maturity I needed for new opportunities and privileges.

Because my friends got to do some things before I did, I could watch and learn from what they did right and wrong.

It was beyond hard to be thankful then, and in fact, I struggled to not become angry. But now I see just as His word says, He was my help and He helped me to not slip into situations I wasn't ready for.

LIVING CHERISHED

Are there some privileges you wish you had, but are not old enough for yet? How might God be working in your life, watching over you, so that you don't slip as you are growing up?

....

....

....

TALKING WITH GOD

God, this is one part of growing up that I am not a fan of; waiting for the things I want to do now. Thank You for overseeing every part of my life and for helping and protecting me every day. In Jesus' name, amen.

DAY 60

FOLLOWING BEHIND

MICHELLE

*The LORD himself goes before you and will be
with you; he will never leave you nor forsake
you. Do not be afraid; do not be discouraged.*
DEUTERONOMY 31:8 NIV

For a lot of people, being the first person to try something
is scary. They want someone else to try it first so they can
watch.

When I was in middle school, I used to wish I had an older
brother or sister like some of my friends. They seemed to know
things that I was clueless about. What to wear, what class was
best, and which teacher was the nicest were just a few things
they had the inside scoop on. I felt that it made life a little
easier. I so wanted to have someone that I could follow behind.

Did you know that in the Bible, it tells us that God actually
goes before us? It amazes me that I can follow behind Him,
and He will guide me with wisdom and insight if I connect
with Him and ask Him to show me the way. That idea makes
me feel brave! Like I can do anything—even something new.
Or go anywhere—maybe somewhere I've never been before.

Recently, it took me a while to commit to a trip. I realized
it was because I'm a little nervous about going by myself! I'm
so grateful that I won't actually be alone when I go because
God not only has already been there, but He'll be with me as I
travel. His help and guidance are literally just a prayer away.

LIVING CHERISHED

Take some alone time today and write about or draw a place you've always wanted to go or a thing you've always wanted to try. Now put God in the picture going before you and then walking beside you, talking you through this new experience.

....

....

....

TALKING TO GOD

God, help me believe that no matter where I go or what I try, You've already gone ahead of me. Empower me to relax, let You lead, and enjoy new things, knowing You are right by my side. In Jesus' name, amen.

FOR MY GOOD

Lynn

My son, keep your father's command and do not forsake your mother's teaching. Bind them always on your heart; fasten them around your neck. When you walk, they will guide you; when you sleep, they will watch over you; when you awake, they will speak to you.

PROVERBS 6:20–22 NIV

It is no secret that every family is different. We have different traditions, beliefs, and rules. My parents seemed to have the strictest rules. They had rules about the places I could go and who I could go with. There were chores that had to be done, clothes I couldn't wear, and music I couldn't listen to.

Many of those rules were different from the rules that my friends' families had, and sometimes this made me angry. I couldn't see the reason behind the rules.

I wish I had known Proverbs 6:20–22 because it might have helped. These verses say, "My son, keep your father's command and do not forsake your mother's teaching. Bind them always on your heart; fasten them around your neck. When you walk, they will guide you; when you sleep, they will watch over you; when you awake, they will speak to you."

All those rules my parents put in place were to protect me. Obeying my parents taught me an even greater principle—I learned how to obey Father God. Now, when God asks me to do something that I don't really want to do or seems hard, I have already learned that rules given by someone who loves me are for my good. They're meant to guide me, watch over me, and lead me. And you know what? Structure actually makes me feel secure.

LIVING CHERISHED

What are some rules in your life that you struggle with? Why might these rules be for your good?

....

....

....

TALKING WITH GOD

Lord, sometimes I struggle with authority figures like my parents who try to teach me. Please help me to be humble and teachable, knowing that what I learn from them will guide and help me to go in the right direction. In Jesus' name, amen.

CELEBRATING GOOD THINGS

MICHELLE

For the LORD God is a sun and shield; the LORD bestows favor and honor; no good thing does he withhold from those whose walk is blameless.

PSALM 84:11 NIV

What good things could you celebrate in your life today? When it's been a tough day, I tend to focus on what went wrong and feel like the whole world is against me. When these days happen, I try and remind myself of the good things in my life.

Sometimes, though, my ability to recall anything good escapes me. Then I'll call a great friend like my sister and ask her to remind me of the good things I'm forgetting. Usually as we're talking, she will also remind me of the good things I have to look forward to, like finishing an assignment or a fun trip our family has already planned.

The Bible says in Psalm 84 that God is our sun. He's a bright warm light that can shine on our dark days and make them brighter. He is also a shield providing protection from letting one tough day take over our thoughts and feelings. He promises to lift us up, but it helps if we talk to Him so He can remind us of this truth.

What do you need from God today? He promises to be your sun, a shield to give you grace, lift you up, and withhold nothing good from you. He truly wants to give you the experience of an amazing life filled with His goodness.

LIVING CHERISHED

Write out a few really good things about your life on the lines below, like how God is a bright sun even on our darkest days. Bookmark this page so when you're having a tough day, you can remind yourself of all of the ways God blesses and protects you.

....

....

....

TALKING WITH GOD

God, I want to believe Your goodness can light up even the hard days and that You shield my heart when I feel hurt. Thanks for Your promises. Send me reminders of them so I won't forget. In Jesus' name, amen.

SHARING JESUS' LOVE

Lynn

Some men came carrying a paralyzed man on a mat and tried to take him into the house to lay him before Jesus. When they could not find a way to do this because of the crowd, they went up on the roof and lowered him on his mat through the tiles into the middle of the crowd, right in front of Jesus.

LUKE 5:18–19 NIV

Have you ever watched another person get picked on or made fun of?

I am very sorry to say that I have. In 4th grade, there was a boy in our class who wore pants that were just too big for him. I don't know if it was because he had to wear hand-me-downs from a brother but his pants just didn't fit him right.

I could have stood up for him and been the one to make the other kids leave him alone, but I didn't. I was afraid. I think if I had really known how much Jesus loved me, He could've used me to pass that love on to another.

There were some guys in the Bible who had a friend who was different from other people too. Their friend was disabled and couldn't walk. I'm sure there were times when people made fun of him as well. These guys were real friends, though. They took their friend to Jesus because they knew Jesus could heal him.

It wasn't easy. In order to get to Jesus, they had to carry their friend up onto a roof and begin pulling the roof apart to create a hole big enough to lower their friend down.

Would someone yell at them for breaking the roof? For sure! Would others tell them to leave Jesus alone? Probably.

But these friends had seen something in Jesus that they knew would make all of the difference in their friend's life. He loved people. His love healed people and they loved their friend enough to get him to Jesus.

That is the kind of girl I want to be. I want to be a girl who understands how much Jesus loves me. I want others to know and experience that love, even when it costs me something. It will cost me time and energy. It might even cost me other friends. But it's worth it to help others know and experience the love of Jesus.

LIVING CHERISHED

Below, write a list of seven people you know who need to experience the love of Jesus. Choose to pray for one person each day this week.

....

....

....

TALKING TO GOD

Jesus, thank You so much for Your powerful love that changes people. Thank You for changing me. Make me bold so that I will share with others that they too are loved and cherished. In Jesus' name, amen.

BOSS YOUR THOUGHTS

LYNN

I will sing of your love and justice; to you,
LORD, I will sing praise.

PSALM 101:1 NIV

Y ou know those days when you wake up and you're just not feeling it? You don't feel like going to school. You don't feel like taking a shower, brushing your teeth, or eating breakfast.

Today had the potential to be one of those days. As soon as my eyes opened, my brain tried to be negative. I'm learning that I have to be the boss of my thoughts and not let them be the boss of me.

I headed down to my favorite chair to spend some time with Jesus and this is what I read:

"I will sing of your love and justice; to you, LORD, I will sing praise" (Psalm 101:1). You know the words that stood out to me?

I will.

David said, "I *will* sing of your love . . . I *will* sing praise." He is making a choice about what he is going to do. He may or may not feel like it, but either way, he is going to sing of God's love and praise Him.

God is holy, perfect, mighty, and good. Praise is what He deserves as our God. We sing praises because we have chosen Him as our Savior and Lord. This isn't the only reason to sing of His love, though! When we sing words that praise God and talk about His love for us, our mind and heart hear the words our mouth is saying and we believe the words we are singing. These words of love reinforce the truth we need to hear over and over again . . . I am loved! When we sing of God's love, these words remind our brain that we are loved and it causes us to feel good inside.

I read an article once that said this is true; music releases a chemical in our brain that helps us feel good! I am always amazed when science backs up what God has already told us in His word!

This one simple choice—paying attention to the music we sing and choosing good songs—can make a huge difference in not only *knowing* we are loved, but *feeling* it as well.

LIVING CHERISHED

Ask a friend, parent, or other cherished person in your life what her favorite songs are that talk about God's love for us and jot them down below. Then share your favorite songs with her. If you have devices that play music, create your own "We Are Loved" playlist together!

....

....

....

TALKING WITH GOD

God, thank You for creating music so we can use it to praise You. When I do, my heart is filled with Your love! In Jesus' name, amen.

WHITE AS SNOW

LYNN

*"Come now, let us settle the matter," says the
LORD. "Though your sins are like scarlet, they
shall be as white as snow; though they are
red as crimson, they shall be like wool."*
ISAIAH 1:18 NIV

I often knew as soon as I woke up whether or not the weatherman had been right. There was a quietness about those days. I would run to my bedroom window to see if it was true and there, I would be greeted by the most beautiful sight.

I couldn't get out into it fast enough, especially if school was cancelled. If it was still falling, I would stick out my mitten, catch some fresh flakes, and look as closely as I could. It was mysterious to me, mind-boggling actually, to think that God would design something so intricate, so absolutely beautiful, in something so very tiny. I would guess most people have no idea just how gorgeous a single flake is! This beauty covers everything.

Pure, white snow.

God says He does this and so much more with my sin. When I come to Him, He covers over my sin. He replaces what was ugly with what is beautiful—His love.

This brings so much peace to my heart. I am free for good from holding the weight of the guilt it has caused. Because of Jesus, you and I are whiter than snow!

LIVING CHERISHED

How does it make you feel to know that God is so willing to wipe all of your sin away? Relieved? Happy? Something else? Write it out below, along with a short prayer of thanks to Him.

....

....

....

TALKING WITH GOD

God, thank You for Your willingness to forgive me for my sin. I just can't thank You enough! In Jesus' name, amen.

SECTION 3

I AM SECURE

Meditation Matters Verses

"For God has not given us a spirit of fear, but of power and of love and of a sound mind."

2 TIMOTHY 1:7 NKJV

"Truly, I tell you, if anyone says to this mountain, 'Go, throw yourself into the sea,' and does not doubt in their heart but believes that what they say will happen, it will be done for them."

MARK 11:23 NIV

". . . neither height nor depth, nor anything else in all creation, will be able to separate us from the love of God that is in Christ Jesus our Lord."

ROMANS 8:39 NIV

ONLY GOD IS GOOD

Lynn

You are good and do only good; teach me your decrees.

PSALM 119:68 NLT

One of the things I enjoy most in my life is getting to be mom to three great kids. I love my kids so much, and I have always tried my hardest to be a really good mom.

No matter how hard I try though, there have been days when I haven't been a good mom. There have been days when I have lost my temper, said things that were unkind, and even a day when I forgot to pick up my daughter from school! (Can you even imagine how unhappy she was with me that day?)

Psalm 119:68 tells us something absolutely amazing about God: "You are good and do only good." God is good; He is blameless, pure, and honest. Not only is God good, but He can only do good.

There will be those days when life is not good. Like me, there might be days when your parent is upset with you and you didn't deserve it. You might not get the grade you expected, make the team, or get invited to that party. Good seems far from your life. Yet even on these types of days, we can trust that God is still good and He will only be good to us.

Some days this is hard to understand. When He doesn't answer my prayers (at least the way I want) or bad things just won't stop happening, I can be tempted to wonder where God is and why He isn't helping me. It's at times like these that it is so important to know what His Word says when God doesn't make sense. God is good and God can only do good.

LIVING CHERISHED

Is there something in your life right now that is making you feel super uneasy? Maybe you're wondering what God is up to. Write about it below and give it to Him. Then ask an adult you know who also loves Jesus if there has been a time in his/her life when they didn't understand why something was happening.

....

....

....

TALKING WITH GOD

God, _____ is hurting me. (Fill in the blank with your own pain.) Your Word says that You are good and You can only do good. Even if I can't see that right now, help me to trust that this is true. In Jesus' name, amen.

JESUS WILL NEVER TURN YOU AWAY

LYNN

All that the Father gives me will come to me,
and whoever comes to me I will never cast out.
JOHN 6:37 ESV

I love reading books about Jesus. They encourage me and help me understand Him better. Do you know what is even better though? Reading Jesus' actual words for ourselves.

In John 6:37 Jesus says, "All that the Father gives me will come to me, and whoever comes to me I will never cast out." Jesus Himself says, "I will never cast you out." He says He will never drive us away; never reject us. He will never turn away anyone who comes to Him.

Never.

He never turns His back because He has lost patience with us. When we come to Him, whether it is because we are so happy we could explode or because we are so sad our heart is breaking, He is there. His arms are open wide to take us in . . . always. He made us, so He understands us better than anyone else.

Not only will Jesus never leave us, He gives us gifts when we come to Him; gifts of eternal life, living with Him forever, and the gift of forgiveness to make us clean and whole.

I get a big smile on my face just picturing this! We come to Him and He greets us with His unconditional love.

When Jesus spoke these words, He was giving us words to assure us that He wants us to come and when we do, He'll be waiting right there. He tells us that everyone who looks to Him and believes in Him shall have eternal life (v. 40).

LIVING CHERISHED

Speak these words out loud so your heart and mind can hear this truth: Jesus will *never* turn me away. Who else do you think needs to hear this truth? How can you share Jesus' welcoming love with them or pray for them this week?

....

....

....

TALKING WITH GOD

Jesus, the way You love me is simply amazing. Thank You that You will never leave me or turn away from me. Thank You that there is nothing I could do to ever make You cast me away. In Jesus' name, amen.

DREAMING BIG

MICHELLE

*"For I know the plans I have for you," declares
the LORD, "plans to prosper you and not to
harm you, plans to give you hope and a future."*
JEREMIAH 29:11 NIV

Have you ever been in school or laid on your bed and dreamed about a different life? One where maybe you were smarter, funnier, better at sports, or had more friends. I remember seeing kids' lives on TV and wishing my life was more like theirs. While comparing ourselves to someone else can sometimes cause us problems, dreaming about a better life can be the start of great thoughts and choices that can change our future.

You were made to dream and chase after good things. As you grow up, you will make choices that will either launch you toward great things or create detours down a not so good path. I want to encourage you to write down your dreams no matter how silly it may seem to do so. I remember writing when I was in 3rd and 7th grade that I would someday like to be a writer, and today you are reading my written words!

I have friends who, every day, write down dreams they hope come true 10 years from now. In 10 years, you will be an adult (or close to it!) living the life you have chosen with the freedom to create an amazing life for yourself.

What do you want your adult life to look like someday? Write it down and know it's OK if your dreams change as you get older. I know many of my dreams seemed crazy, and the paths my life took made very little sense to me at the time. As I've gotten older and look back, I can now see an amazing plan unfolding that I could have never created on my own. I'm so grateful I never gave up on my dreams because when the time was right, I was ready! You will be too.

LIVING CHERISHED

Write down a dream you have about your future, and then write or say a prayer of thanksgiving that God's dreams for your life are even bigger and better than the dreams you have for yourself!

....

....

....

TALKING WITH GOD

God, thank You for having great plans for me. Help me look to You and remember I have hope and a future, even on the tough days. In Jesus' name, amen.

WHERE I GOT IT RIGHT AND WHERE I GOT IT WRONG

LYNN

Very truly I tell you, whoever hears my word and believes him who sent me has eternal life and will not be judged but has crossed over from death to life.

JOHN 5:24 NIV

Many weeks at church looked the same for me. At the end of the service, our pastor would ask, "Would you like to have Jesus forgive you for your sin and give you a new life?" In my heart, I knew that I had sinned that week and needed Jesus to forgive me. So I went up to the front of the church and prayed the prayer to begin a relationship with Jesus *again*.

There was a part of me that got this right, but there was a bigger part of me that had it all wrong.

You and I sin. I wish it wasn't so, but because we are human, we make decisions and choices that aren't right. We all need forgiveness.

Here is God's promise about the forgiveness we need . . . "If we confess our sins, he is faithful and just to forgive us our sins and to cleanse us from all unrighteousness" (1 John 1:9 ESV). If we admit to God that we have sinned, He forgives us and wipes us clean from it all! That is the best news ever!

Here's the part I got wrong: we don't have to begin a new relationship with Jesus whenever we sin. If we believe Jesus is God's Son and have given Him our life, we have already received that new life, there are no do-overs needed.

LIVING CHERISHED

There may be times in your life when, because of your sin, you don't *feel* like you are a child of God. Remember that if you have already asked Jesus into your heart, you only need to ask for forgiveness. If you know of sin in your life right now, ask Jesus to forgive you specifically for that sin—then thank Him for the blessing of forgiveness!

....

....

....

TALKING WITH GOD

God, thank You so much for forgiving me each time I come to You and admit my sin. Thank you for forgiving me for _____. In Jesus' name, amen.

JUST GO FOR IT!

LYNN

. . . for the LORD is your security. He will keep your foot from being caught in a trap.

PROVERBS 3:26 NLT

Do you like to try new things? Sometimes I do; sometimes I don't. If I think it's going to be fun and I'll be good at it, then no problem! Let's go for it. But . . . if there is a chance that I might fail, not so much.

This type of thinking, if I let it stick around, can cause me to miss out on some really great opportunities. If the chance of failure is the thing that is holding me back, I'll be held back a lot!

But we don't have to be afraid to try new things! Proverbs 3:26 tells us that the Lord is our security; He is our freedom from care, anxiety, or doubt. He gives us the confidence we need to overcome scary things.

Reading this truth makes me feel stronger already! His Word helps me find the courage to take a deep breath and go for it, whatever it might be. His love for me helps me know that even if I do fail, it doesn't change the way He looks at me or sees me. In fact, God might even use failing for good! I just might learn something new in taking the risk.

What God won't allow is for me to be alone. This verse says, "He will keep your foot from being caught in a trap." There is nothing that can cause me to become stuck and without His help. There is not a situation that God can't or won't help me with because of His great love for me. Will it be easy? Most times it isn't! But no matter what, He is with me and He is for me.

LIVING CHERISHED

Think about and write down some things you would like to try if you knew there was no way you could fail. Take some time to pray and ask the Lord if there's something on your list that He would like you to try, even if you mess up or don't get everything right the first time.

....
....
....

TALKING WITH GOD

God, I don't want fear, especially fear of failure, to hold me back from trying new things. I know that You have great things for me in my future and I want to be secure, knowing that wherever I go and whatever I do, You are with me! In Jesus' name, amen.

LOST AND FOUND

LYNN

"And when he has found it, he will joyfully carry it home on his shoulders. When he arrives, he will call together his friends and neighbors, saying, 'Rejoice with me because I have found my lost sheep.'"

LUKE 15:5–6 NLT

In Luke 15, Jesus tells the story of a man who has 100 sheep and loses one. He leaves the other 99 sheep to go after the one that is lost and he keeps looking until he finds it. When he finds it, he puts the sheep on his shoulders, so happy to be carrying her home.

When he gets home, he calls all of his friends and neighbors over to celebrate with him.

Jesus tells us this is the way God feels when one of us, who was lost and not in a relationship with Him, is found. He throws a party!

God is not ashamed of the one who wandered away. Instead, He says, "I have found *my* lost sheep." He celebrates that the one He loves is back. That is God's heart of love. He doesn't push away the one that ran or drag her back home. Instead, He draws her close, joyfully putting her on his shoulders. He wants us as close to Him as we can be!

Isn't this type of love amazing?

Through God's actions of pure love, He's teaching us how we should love others. When we see another wander away or go astray, we are not to kick them on their way out, talk behind their backs, or judge them for the choices they are making. Love goes after them, just like the Shepherd. Love goes "in search of the one that went astray."

You and I are called to treat others like God treats us, and He wants none of His children lost!

LIVING CHERISHED

Do you know someone in your life who might have gone astray? Ask Jesus how you can show them His unconditional love so they will know it too! Write out a prayer to Him here.

....

....

....

TALKING WITH GOD

Lord, thank You for loving me perfectly even when I am far from perfect. Fill me with Your love so I can love others this way too! In Jesus' name, amen.

NO LONGER INVISIBLE

Lynn

*She gave this name to the LORD who spoke to
her: "You are the God who sees me," for she
said, "I have now seen the One who sees me."*

GENESIS 16:13 NIV

Have you ever switched schools? I did several times; going
into 3rd grade, going into 7th grade, and going into 10th
grade. If you have, too, I wonder if you experienced what I
experienced. The friend groups were already set. Kids noticed
the new girl, then forgot her just as fast. They already had their
friends, they didn't really need more.

You feel invisible.

One thing I have come to love about reading my Bible is
finding people in it who felt like I feel and God has helped them.

In Genesis 16, there is a woman named Hagar. She and
another woman named Sarai had gotten in a huge fight because
Sarai was jealous of Hagar. Sarai's jealousy was so powerful
she couldn't even stand to look at Hagar. Sarai treated Hagar
so badly, Hagar ran away!

Out in the middle of the desert, Hagar felt lonely and for-
gotten. Here, the Angel of the Lord shows up to comfort her!
Stunned by His appearance and words, Genesis 16:13 says:
"She gave this name to the LORD who spoke to her: 'You are the
God who sees me,' for she said, 'I have now seen the One who
sees me.'"

Jesus understands what it's like to feel invisible; forgotten. The night before He died on the cross, some of His closest friends deserted Him.

Like He did with Hagar, God sees you. He sees the hard things you are going through in life. He knows all about your family trouble, those things you are so scared of, and how hard you're struggling in school. He sees you. He loves you. He is with you.

LIVING CHERISHED

When have you felt invisible? Picture yourself in that situation and write or draw it below. Now say out loud to yourself, "God sees you." This may feel weird, but when we take the time to picture what was *really* happening in our situations, how we were not alone, it can help to heal the part of us that is hurting. How does your story or picture change when you realize that God is always with you?

....

....

....

TALKING WITH GOD

Thank You, God, that no matter where I am and no matter what I am going through, You see me. In Jesus' name, amen.

NO MORE ANXIETY

MICHELLE

Cast all your anxiety on him because
he cares for you.

1 PETER 5:7 NIV

"Mom, you don't understand the stress I feel."

She's right. I don't. I don't walk in her shoes, I don't attend her school, and I've never been friends with her classmates. Stress comes from two places in life. There's outside stress, like other people's words and actions and difficult situations. And there's inside stress, created by the thoughts we think and what we choose to value each day.

Wouldn't it be great if we could just throw away our worries that lead to anxiety? Actually, God's word says we can cast—meaning to "throw forcefully"—our cares on God. We can just pitch all of them at Him and He will catch them. I like using a "worry box" to hold the worries I write down to remind me God has them.

God takes our worries because He cares for us.

I'll be honest. I have days when my kids are tired or busy and my husband who travels is out of town and I wonder for just a second, "Does anyone really care what happened to me today?" Then I remind myself that God does! He not only catches our worries, but He replaces them with positive promises.

LIVING CHERISHED

What are some worries that you can give to God? Write them out here or create a "worry catcher" box. We make these in our counseling center using Kleenex boxes. Clients write their worries on slips of paper and leave them behind. Try leaving at least one worry a day in your box. When it gets full, dump it out and thank God as you let go of more and more worries.

....

....

....

TALKING TO GOD

God, thanks for caring about my worries both large and small. Help me to cast them far away from my mind and give them to You. Thanks for always being there. In Jesus' name, amen.

FOR EVER AND EVER

LYNN

But the love of the LORD remains forever with those who fear him. His salvation extends to the children's children.

PSALM 103:17 NLT

Have you ever had someone you love leave this earth? It can be very painful when someone you care about dies.

When I was a young woman, my father passed away. It was a very hard time for me. When I was a little girl, my father was very quiet. On top of that, he worked a lot of hours. While I believed my dad loved me, I really wanted to hear him say it. I wanted so much for him to be the type of daddy that would pick me up, kiss me, and snuggle me in my bed. But he wasn't that type of daddy. He was strong, dependable, but not sensitive like I wanted.

So when he died, there was a part of me that really felt lost. Now I would never have what I wanted so badly.

As I have grown closer and closer to God, my heavenly Father, I have felt this hurting part of me healing. When I read verses like Psalm 103:17, where it says that "the love of the LORD remains forever with those who fear him," it's a soothing medicine on my heart.

God loves us, friend. His love will never leave us and will never die. His love remains forever because *He remains forever!* It's everlasting, endless, and permanent. My heart needs to know this truth. Does yours?

164

LIVING CHERISHED

One thing that helps me really understand and allow God's love to soak into my heart is music that speaks of Him. In fact, I have a playlist of songs called "His Love" filled with songs that specifically talk about God's great love for me. What are some things that remind you of God's love for you? Maybe it's a playlist, a book like this one, or conversations with an adult who loves Jesus and loves you!

....
....
....

TALKING WITH GOD

Father God, I am so grateful for a love like Yours that truly is eternal. Thank You! In Jesus' name, amen.

LOVING THE "UNLOVABLE"

LYNN

Jesus reached out his hand and touched the man. "I am willing," he said. "Be clean!" And immediately the leprosy left him.

LUKE 5:13 NIV

In Luke 5:12, we meet a man with leprosy—a serious skin disease that causes a person to have sores all over their body. It was extremely contagious. If you touched someone with this disease, chances are you would get it as well. For this reason, people with this disease were sent away from their family, friends, and community.

Yet, here in this verse, Jesus, reaches out and touches this sick man on purpose! His actions proved to the man that he was not unlovable.

The dictionary says that the word "unlovable" is a real word, but according to God's Word, I don't think it is. The definition of unlovable means to literally be *not lovable*.

But that's impossible! When He was on the earth Jesus demonstrated He loves everyone!

He showed love to those who were sick. He loved those who were choosing to sin, showing them a new way to live. He loved those who made mistakes, thinking they were living right, but they weren't.

There may be days for you, when you feel unlovable. Someone's actions or words may make you feel that you are too bad to be loved. That's just not true!

It's impossible to be unlovable. Tuck this truth away in your heart.

LIVING CHERISHED

Have you ever felt unlovable? If so, think back to that time and write down the feelings that come up. Now shut your eyes and say out loud to yourself, "I am loved." I know it feels weird and silly, but your heart needs to hear this truth. Your heart believes your words, so cheer it on! How did your feelings change after speaking God's truth out loud? Write down those feelings.

....

....

....

TALKING WITH GOD

God, thank You that according to You, "unlovable" does not exist. Thank You that there is nothing I could ever do to make You not love me! In Jesus' name, amen.

WHAT DOES IT TAKE?

LYNN

The LORD delights in those who fear him,
who put their hope in his unfailing love.
PSALM 147:11 NIV

Have you ever thought about what it takes to make God happy with you? This is a question I wrestled with a lot. Oh, I don't say it out loud. These are the thoughts I've had. Since I didn't know the answer, I assumed I would have to be perfect in order for Him to not be mad or disappointed in me.

Guess what? I was so wrong! That is what happens when we don't know the truth in God's Word. We can get the answers to the questions in our minds wrong.

In Psalm 147:11 it says that in order for God to delight in me, or take a high level of enjoyment in me, it's simple. He is very pleased with those who fear him, those who respect Him, and those who put their hope in His unfailing love.

I don't find it difficult to respect God. I'm in awe of the way He made me, made the earth, and of the power He has over it all. But sometimes it can be hard for me to hope in His unfailing love. I naturally lean more toward hoping in other people to do what I want or give me what I need. I believe that if I study enough, work hard enough, or just don't mess up, things will turn out OK. But not only does that not always work; that type of hope doesn't please God. He wants me to hope in Him . . . in His love that will never fail me.

It can be hard to hope in a love that we can't see. God isn't physically standing right beside us, putting His arms around us. He isn't physically speaking words in our ears that make us feel better after something sad has happened or we have had a bad day.

This is where faith comes in. We believe, based on the truth we have found in His Word, that we can trust Him. His love is perfect; it cannot fail us. His love might not always do everything the way we want or the way we expect, but He will always act toward us in a way that is best *for* us.

Always.

That is the definition of unfailing love. It cannot let us down or let us go.

LIVING CHERISHED

Remind yourself that you can hope in God's unfailing love. Write or draw something below that can remind you of this hope, like a song lyric, a smiling face, a sunbeam, a prayer, or something else, and then bookmark this page so you can come back to it whenever you need it.

....

....

....

TALKING WITH GOD

Lord, thank You for not being hard to please. Not everyone in my life is like You in this way. Help me remember that no matter what I do, You love me with unfailing love. In Jesus' name, amen.

EYES FOR YOU

LYNN

*But the LORD watches over all who honor
him and trust his kindness.*

PSALM 33:18 CEV

You know that feeling you get when you sense someone is staring at you? I immediately try to figure out why. *What are they looking at? Is there something wrong with my hair? Did I spill food on my shirt? Is there something stuck between my teeth?*

We usually think that someone is staring at us because something is wrong. This is the opposite of how and why God is watching over us. In Psalm 33:18, God says He is staring at us because of something good! He watches over all who honor Him and trust in His kindness. (Notice what it doesn't say. It doesn't say that He watches over those who *hope* they are good enough!)

As we worship Him, the Lord is watching over and protecting us. He wants to take care of us and keep us from harm. His eyes are on us because we honor Him and trust that He wants only good for us.

When I read these words, it helps me know that I am loved and protected. Knowing He is looking at me and watching out for me gives me comfort, especially on the days I feel alone or even invisible.

No matter what happens today, if it's the best day ever or absolutely horrible, you can know that the way God sees you doesn't change. He loves you. He is watching you with eyes of love, never with eyes that are mad, annoyed, or disappointed. I know that's hard to believe because others in our lives—teachers, coaches, even parents—do look at us like that from time to time.

But God is different. He is perfect. He sees that you love Him, even if you, your day, or the people in your life aren't perfect.

LIVING CHERISHED

Remind yourself today: God's eyes of love are on me! Name a few good things God sees when He sees you.

....

....

....

TALKING WITH GOD

God, thank You that You are looking at me all the time with Your eyes of love. In Jesus' name, amen.

ALL MY FEARS

LYNN

*I sought the LORD and He answered me
and delivered me from all my fears.*
PSALM 34:4 ESV

Will I ever fit in?

I had my doubts. So many things about me were different from those around me.

My body seemed so far behind others. Though I wore a bra, I didn't need to. (The guys were quick to point that out!)

My personality seemed to continually gush out of me. Talking, laughing, even snorting when I laughed, I was the girl who was rarely quiet, even when I was supposed to be. Often, I felt I couldn't control the out-of-control me.

"In" just didn't seem to be a thing I was ever going to be. Afraid "different" would follow me all the way to high school, I just wanted to be normal.

I know this may sound strange, but even though I'm all grown up, some days I still just want to be normal. I experience fear that my life won't look like other people's lives . . . or at least the lives they seem to have on social media.

This morning, I read Psalm 34:4: "I prayed to the LORD, and he answered me. He freed me from all my fears" (NLT). This verse gives me hope. Not hope that God will take away my problems, but hope that He will comfort me and bring me relief from the things I fear.

Like me, you have your own list of fears. They might not look like mine. Your list may include the fear that your family will never be all right, you won't get the grades you want, or that kids will never stop teasing you. Take comfort in what I'm taking comfort in—things right now might feel like a mess, but God is right there with you. He can give you the comfort and courage you need today by knowing you are cherished, right there in the middle of it all. You can trust Him to be with you and help you take one day at a time, even one hour or a minute at a time, while you count on Him to help you.

LIVING CHERISHED

Fill in the blanks below with some responses to this sentence: "I prayed to the Lord, and he answered me. He freed me from my fear of _____." Pick your favorite response and write out your personalized reminder in your school agenda, on your phone, or on an index card to keep in your pocket for when your heart feels fearful.

....

....

....

TALKING TO GOD

Lord, thank You that I can give You my fears, and in turn You give me comfort. In Jesus' name, amen.

BEST DAD EVER

LYNN

A father to the fatherless, a defender of widows,
is God in his holy dwelling. God sets the lonely
in families . . .

PSALM 68:5–6A NIV

When the phone rang, my mom yelled that the call was actually for me. I was really excited because I was waiting for my friend Tammy to call and say whether or not her mom would let her go to the high school football game that night. As soon as I said "Hi," Tammy said, "My dad died today."

Her dad died? I had never known anyone who died. Being a 4th grader, I didn't know anyone who had their father die, or even a father who had left because of a divorce. I knew Tammy was hurting, but I didn't know what to say while she was hurting.

After her dad died, life got very hard for my friend. Not having her father left a big gap in her life. She missed him being there to love her.

When someone dies, or for some reason is no longer in our lives, the pain can be great and deep. We might wonder why God let something like that happen to us. *Doesn't He love us?*

Later in my life, when my own daddy died, I didn't have any friends who understood the pain I was going through either. They all had their dads. I felt very alone. In this place of great sadness, I cried to God about how I was hurting.

In Psalm 68, David describes how God is a father to the fatherless. The psalmist says "God sets the lonely in families" (v. 68). One way that He did that for me was giving me a father in my husband's dad when I got married. God shows love, tenderness, and kindness, especially toward the helpless and vulnerable, who for whatever reason don't have the love of an earthly father that they need.

This verse has brought me comfort in the years since my dad died. When the thought that he would no longer be on this earth to be with me hurt so much, I could remember that I had a heavenly Father who loved me. While we can't see or touch our heavenly Father, we can still experience the love that comes from Him.

A love that is perfect for us and provides protection for us. He is a father who will never, ever leave us.

LIVING CHERISHED

One of the things that really helped me when I was sad was to talk to someone. I just needed to get all my emotions off my chest. Write down the names of some adults you can talk to and share your feelings with if you're feeling sad.

....

....

....

TALKING WITH GOD

God, thank You that You are a father who is, and always will be, with me. I'm so very grateful for Your love. I really need You in my life. In Jesus' name, amen.

HE'S GOT YOU

Lynn

> But now, this is what the LORD says—he who
> created you, Jacob, he who formed you, Israel:
> "Do not fear, for I have redeemed you; I have
> summoned you by name; you are mine. When
> you pass through the waters, I will be with you;
> and when you pass through the rivers, they will
> not sweep over you. When you walk through
> the fire, you will not be burned; the flames will
> not set you ablaze."
>
> ISAIAH 43:1–2 NIV

You know one thing I didn't expect growing up? I didn't think there would be parts of my life that would be hard. I began loving Jesus when I was about 8 years old. My mom shared with me how much Jesus loved me, and I heard the same thing at Vacation Bible School. I wanted to love Him too. Somehow I thought that once I started loving Jesus and following the wisdom He gave me in His Word, life would go smoothly. I didn't expect any bumps in the road, as long as I obey His Word.

You know what? That's not what the Bible says. There is nowhere in God's Word where He says life for those who love Him will go perfectly as planned. In fact, Isaiah 43:1–2 surprises those of us who think this way.

In this verse, there is a really important word used three times: *when*.

It doesn't say *if*, but *when* you go through situations that seem beyond what you can take, *when* you go through difficulty, and *when* you walk through times that are hard and life feels cruel. *When* this happens to you, you are still His. *When* it comes, He will be with you. *When* you feel overcome, it will not be the end of you. Don't be afraid, you are God's and He's got you.

You may have already been through some really hard things in life. Maybe it was the divorce of your parents, the death of a grandparent, or the pain of leaving a school you loved. You may be in this place right now. Sweet friend, remember this: God wants you to know that you are His. He's got you and He's with you no matter what.

LIVING CHERISHED

What hard times have you already experienced in your life? Did you know that God was with you during that time? Reread today's verse and help reinforce to your heart that you are His and He calls you by name. How will you remember this truth the next time you go through something hard?

....

....

....

TALKING WITH GOD

God, I get that going through difficulty is part of living here on Earth. Thank You that I will not go through it alone. Thank You for creating me, rescuing me, and calling me by name. In Jesus' name, amen.

NEVER DISTRACTED

LYNN

Since you are precious and honored in my sight, and because I love you, I will give people in exchange for you, nations in exchange for your life.

ISAIAH 43:4 NIV

W*hy won't she put her phone down?*
I had been looking forward to this day for so long, but now that we were together, it's like we weren't. My friend answered my questions, but she wasn't really *with* me. Whatever she was scrolling through was definitely more important than me.

Research says that when we have our phone out, people around us feel they can't really talk. Any moment a ding can pull our person away, so we just keep our conversations shallow.

Honestly, I have been guilty of the same.

I use the words "Love you!" or "Miss you!" but then my actual actions don't really back those words up. When God speaks, His words are not empty like mine can be. They have true meaning and action to back them up.

In Isaiah 43:4, God tells us we are precious, prized to the point that He has given everything to prove His love for us. His words are a promise fulfilled. In the first half of the Bible He said He would send a savior to set us free from our sins; in the second half He did it.

God never says one thing and does another.

Others may delay or be distracted in showing us their love. God never is. His eyes are forever on us, looking at the one who is precious to Him.

LIVING CHERISHED

It's so easy to get distracted. Let's challenge ourselves today to give our full attention to others when they are speaking to us, paying attention and looking at them when they are speaking to us. Write down a few times throughout the day you rose to this challenge, then challenge yourself to do it again tomorrow so active listening becomes a habit for you.

....

....

....

TALKING WITH GOD

God, thank You that You are never distracted. Your eyes are on me, and I am safe with You. Help me show this same love to others today. In Jesus' name, amen.

FOR HIS GLORY

LYNN

*. . . everyone who is called by my name, whom I
created for my glory, whom I formed and made.*

ISAIAH 43:7 NIV

Have you ever wondered why you were made? Why God
made you?

It's pretty easy for us to go through each day doing the
things we have to do and the things we love to do. By the time
you fit all that in, what else is there?

In Isaiah 43:7, God is talking to His people, the people of
Israel. At one time, they lived close to each other and wor-
shiped God together. But now, they have spread out and no
longer ask God for His wisdom or live out His ways.

God is calling them to come back to Him. As He does, He
reminds them, "everyone who is called by my name, whom I
created for my glory, whom I formed and made." God is telling
His people that they've been distracted doing whatever they
want in life. As a result, they've gotten far away from Him. But
He still loves them. He still calls them by His name because He
created them to be a shining example to the world of who He
is—a God of love and goodness.

There are definitely things we *need* to do in life and there
are things we *want* to do in life. But in all of that, no matter
our age, we need to remember that we were made to show the
world how great our God is. Let's not be too busy that we forget
why we were created.

LIVING CHERISHED

What kinds of things do you fill your day with? How can you give God glory and shine for Jesus so that others see Him in your life?

....

....

....

TALKING WITH GOD

God, thank You for creating and forming me. Sometimes I forget that the reason I was made was for You. Help me to keep You above all else in my life. In Jesus' name, amen.

FORGIVEN

Lynn

Where is another God like you, who pardons the guilt of the remnant, overlooking the sins of his special people? You will not stay angry with your people forever, because you delight in showing unfailing love. Once again you will have compassion on us. You will trample our sins under your feet and throw them into the depths of the ocean!

MICAH 7:18–19 NLT

My diary entry on this date was small, but I bet my feelings were not.

May 6th: "Julie and I got in a fight."

Fights are the worst! If you're a people pleaser like I've been, you'll do just about anything to avoid fighting! Have you ever hidden in your room when you thought your mom was mad at you? Gone to the bathroom at school to avoid walking into class and seeing your angry friend? Yep . . . I've done those for sure!

What about when we've done something and God has every reason to feel offended? When we have sinned and acted in a way that goes against what He tells us to do?

I love how these verses in Micah make it so we don't have

to guess what God does in this situation. They teach us what God's love for us is like when we offend Him.

Micah 7:18–19 tells us that God is quick to forgive us for our sins. Once He forgives us, God is ready to move past our sins as well as our failures. He doesn't hold a grudge or stay mad, instead He is quick to forgive and forget.

Why would this be, when we've done something that offends Him? It's because it makes Him happy to love us! Loving us is not a burden to Him. It isn't a pain for Him to love us, even when we act unlovable. You see, to Him we can never be unlovable . . . no matter what!

That is the type of love that "casts our sins into the depths of the sea." He will keep sending that love our way over and over and over again.

LIVING CHERISHED

When have you sinned or done something that offended God? If you haven't yet asked Him to forgive you, do so now. If you have, be assured that He has already forgiven you and moved on, so you can too!

....

....

....

TALKING WITH GOD

God, thank You that You do not hold my sins against me or hold a grudge toward me. I'm so very grateful that You are quick to forgive me each and every time. In Jesus' name, amen.

ALWAYS WITH YOU

MICHELLE

Have I not commanded you? Be strong and courageous. Do not be afraid; do not be discouraged, for the LORD your God will be with you wherever you go.

JOSHUA 1:9 NIV

Have you ever felt alone in a room full of people? It can happen. Loneliness can creep up in the weirdest places. I hate that feeling. Don't you? I want to feel loved, included, and that someone cares.

Sometimes when we're really alone, that's when our negative thoughts or "stinkin' thinkin'" can make us feel bad and want to do nothing but lie there or escape by reading books, playing video games, or watching YouTube. Being OK with being alone takes practice. Now that I've practiced going places alone and having a good time, I can go almost anyplace and not be uncomfortable. I still enjoy going with a friend more, but I have the confidence to know I can do it.

Did you know there isn't a single place you can go that God won't go with you? I like to imagine I have an invisible pocket that holds all the love, joy, hope, and peace God has and gives to me so I can carry it around with me. I love reminding myself that the God of the universe is always with me, even though I can't see or touch Him.

LIVING CHERISHED

Each morning, practice waking up and recognizing that God is with you so you can train your brain and spirit to recognize his presence. Over the next few days, write down any changes you notice as you start your days with awareness of His presence.

....

....

....

TALKING WITH GOD

God, thank You for creating me to desire being with people, but also to be comfortable with being alone because You are always with me. Help me believe You truly do go with me wherever I go, even though I cannot see or touch You. In Jesus' name, amen.

GETTING TO KNOW GOD

Lynn

Know that the LORD is God. It is he who made us, and we are his; we are his people, the sheep of his pasture.

PSALM 100:3 NIV

Do you and a friend have a little inside joke, a secret saying only the two of you get?

My family has lots of them; little things we say that remind us of something in the past and get us laughing. In fact, a couple of years ago we got T-shirts made that said, "You wouldn't get it; it's a Cowell thing." While you might not understand what's so funny about the silly language we use or that story we told, we do because we belong to each other.

God longs for us to experience this type of belonging with Him; only deeper. Stronger. He wants us to know Him; to get Him. Yes, there will always be some things about Him that we don't understand. That is part of God being God. There is, however, much about Him that we *can* understand. And He wants us to, beginning with knowing how great, powerful, and mighty He is. Psalm 100:3 starts out, "Know that the Lord is God."

God wants us to know Him. That's why He gave us His Word, the Bible, so we can know Him more.

Just like we want to know about our parents and grand-parents, asking questions about what their life was like before we were born, God wants us to do the same with Him. Because we're part of His family, the more we know about Him, the more we'll love Him.

LIVING CHERISHED

Find a Bible verse that reminds your heart that you are His. Write it down here, and then use it in your prayers throughout the week as a "secret saying" between you and God!

....

....

....

TALKING WITH GOD

God, thank You for giving me the chance to know You. Thank You that You already know and get me fully. I'm so very grateful to be Yours. In Jesus' name, amen.

PIMPLE, PIMPLE, GO AWAY!

LYNN

How beautiful you are, my love; how perfect you are!

SONG OF SOLOMON 4:7 GNT

When I was your age, my January 4th diary entry said, "I'm getting pimples all over my face. It must be because I'm 12! This is the pits!"

Going through body changes isn't for the faint of heart! All too often, the changes aren't the changes we want. Whether it's the shape of our body, getting pimples, or even the new thoughts we think and the feelings that are unpredictable . . . everything seems to be changing all at once.

Sometimes, it can be hard to see these changes as good things. But our Creator sees good when He looks at us.

Song of Solomon 4:7 says, "You are altogether beautiful, my darling, beautiful in every way." He says we are beautiful in *every* way!

He's not just talking about what you see when you look in the mirror.

Think for a moment about all the things that make you "you." Yes, there's your body, but there's also your personality and your mind. You are gorgeous in *every way*.

One thing I enjoy doing when reading my Bible is reading it in different translations. Doing that with this verse helps me understand it even better. Here is Song of Solomon 4:7 in a few translations:

"You are altogether beautiful, my darling; there is no flaw in you" (NIV).

"You are altogether beautiful, my darling, And there is no blemish in you" (NASB).

"You are absolutely beautiful, my darling; there is no imperfection in you" (CSB).

Are you getting the picture?

Beautiful one, you are dazzling, delightful, and drop-dead gorgeous. Tell that to the girl looking back at you in the mirror!

LIVING CHERISHED

Pick your favorite translation above of Song of Solomon 4:7 and write it out here. What are some attributes that God sees when He looks at you, like your kind heart, the talents He gave you, or the compassion you have for others?

....

....

....

TALKING WITH GOD

God, thank You for not only thinking I am gorgeous, but saying it so I can hear it too! In Jesus' name, amen.

YOU'RE BEAUTIFUL

LYNN

. . . and I praise you because of the wonderful way you created me. Everything you do is marvelous! Of this I have no doubt.

PSALM 139:14 CEV

Getting ready to go swimming one day, my friend looked at my thighs. "Those aren't supposed to touch," she informed me. "What are you talking about?" I said. Now she pointed. "Your legs. They aren't supposed to touch." This was news to me! I wasn't what you would call skinny, but I was fine with how my body looked.

I've often gotten comments about what others see when they look at me. My hair is too dark, my arms too hairy, and my teeth too crooked. Maybe you've experienced the same thing. Others may think you're too skinny, your skin is too dark, you're too short, or your hair is too curly. You know the beautiful thing about being loved perfectly by God? We don't have to care what others think of how He created us.

Did you get that? Read it out loud. I'll rewrite for you.

I don't have to care what others think of how God created me. The important phrase here is: *don't have to.*

I can care. I can absolutely care what others think or say about me. I can listen. I can believe their words are true. I could have believed all those things people said. (Add the comments on my chest being flat, which never did change!)

Or . . . I can believe what God said about this girl *He* made. Here is the truth found in Psalm 139:14, ". . . and I praise you because of the wonderful way you created me. Everything you do is marvelous! Of this I have no doubt." You. Me. We are simply marvelous!

So whose opinion is the right opinion? God's. We must remind ourselves—it's wonderful the way I'm created. Red hair, yellow, black, brown, or purple. Black skin, brown skin, white, or a mixture; we're wonderfully complex! With glasses, with braces, and facial flaws too . . . I am absolutely gorgeous and loved on top of it!

LIVING CHERISHED

Say out loud, "I am simply marvelous!" Write down some other truths you can say to yourself the next time someone tries to tell you differently, like "Because God made me, I am beautiful!"

....

....

....

TALKING TO GOD

God, thank You for making marvelous me! Help me to grasp this truth and shut out voices that tell me differently. In Jesus' name, amen.

HE'LL NEVER QUIT

LYNN

. . . being confident of this, that he who began a good work in you will carry it on to completion until the day of Christ Jesus.

PHILIPPIANS 1:6 NIV

You know those days when life is just good?

You have a great day at school, you get along with your brother or sister, and you and your friend haven't had a fight in a long time. Most of all, you are growing in your relationship with Jesus. Every day you are learning more about Him and becoming more like Him. It feels good to feel good!

I love those days too. But even on the days when life isn't perfect, this verse in Philippians 1:6 really encourages me. It tells me that every day of my life, because of His great love for me, Jesus is going to keep doing good work in me. Every day, until the day when I will see Him face-to-face, He is going to be for me, working in my life to help me to become more and more like Him.

He won't ever quit on us. It's a promise He has made to us! And because He won't ever quit, we shouldn't either!

LIVING CHERISHED

Take a minute to look at your life and think about where you see Jesus helping you to become more like Him. Write down a few ideas below. Thank Him that He will keep doing this until the day you two are together!

....

....

....

TALKING WITH GOD

God, thank You so much for this great promise You made to me. You will keep working in my life, making me more and more like You, until the day we are together forever! In Jesus' name, amen.

HE HEALS YOUR HEART

LYNN

The Spirit of the LORD GOD is upon me, because the LORD has anointed me to bring good news to the poor; he has sent me to bind up the brokenhearted, to proclaim liberty to the captives, and the opening of the prison to those who are bound.

ISAIAH 61:1 ESV

My December 17th diary entry says: "At choir practice, our director gave my solo to Julie because it was too low for me. That kind of hurt."

As I read these words written in my diary years ago, my guess is that I wasn't being completely truthful about the way I felt. I didn't get too real, even there. *What if someone read it one day?*

This one situation was part of a string of rejections as I was growing up; being picked last for the team at gym class, not chosen to be his girlfriend, and left out of the party invitation list. For the girl who wanted to be valued and feel worthwhile, the worst possible thing was to not feel that way.

The words in Isaiah 61:1, which describe Jesus, is medicine to our hurting heart. It's like the cool and soothing kind of medicine Mom put on my skinned knee when I wiped out on my bike. Isaiah 61:1 says "He binds up the brokenhearted."

When we endure one rejection, it's not so bad. But when they keep coming over and over again, we find ourselves under the category of brokenhearted . . . smothered under disappointment.

While my mom did a great job with my banged-up knee, only Jesus has been able to bind up my broken heart again and again. His love is exactly what I have needed to repair the hurts that have come my way. Now, I trust Him to do what only He can with His love.

You can trust Him too. You can know, when the blow of rejection comes, exactly where to go. He can pick up the pieces of our hearts, no matter how much they've been broken, and put us back together once more.

LIVING CHERISHED

Have you had a time when you've been brokenhearted? Has your heart healed? Do you need Jesus to work on healing you? Ask Him to begin this work today.

....

....

....

TALKING WITH GOD

Jesus, living in this world can be very painful. There's no way to get around it; it's to be expected. Thank You that when I am hurting, I know that I can come to You. I trust You to heal me completely. In Jesus' name, amen.

STANDING STRONG

LYNN

*. . . and provide for those who grieve in Zion—
to bestow on them a crown of beauty instead of
ashes, the oil of joy instead of mourning, and a
garment of praise instead of a spirit of despair.
They will be called oaks of righteousness, a
planting of the LORD for the display of his
splendor.*

ISAIAH 61:3 NIV

Recently I told a friend, "I would rather get lost in the woods than be found in a mall."

You and I may or may not have this nature-loving side of us in common, but maybe you have a tree or two near where you live. My front yard has so many trees I wouldn't want to count them.

There are tall, slender pines that could snap in half when a blustery storm blows through. The dogwoods burst with beautiful, white blooms every spring.

But standing above them all are the mighty oaks. Known for their strength and stability, our oak trees just grow taller and taller year after year. They have survived the weight of ice storms and winds from hurricane leftovers. They just keep standing, providing shade to the deer who hang out below.

As I read these verses in Isaiah that describe Jesus, I see a list of sorrows from life storms: ashes, mourning, and despair.

I also see what Jesus gives us even when we suffer through these hard times—beauty, joy, and cheer in its place. When Jesus comes with His love into our hurting places, we become healed. Like a mighty oak in Him, we become an example to others of what His love can do. Seeing this causes others to look to Him for the healing and love they need as well.

LIVING CHERISHED

Have you gone through a life storm that has created sadness in your life? Read through Isaiah 61:3, paying close attention to the exchanges Jesus wants to make in your life. Then write or draw what it would be like to be a tall, strong, mighty oak tree in a forest.

....
....
....

TALKING WITH GOD

God, please heal the parts of my heart that feel sad because of
_____. I want to be a girl who displays to the rest of the
world just how strong You are in us. In Jesus' name, amen.

CHOSEN ONE

Lynn

*Therefore, as God's chosen people, holy and
dearly loved, clothe yourselves with compassion,
kindness, humility, gentleness and patience.*

COLOSSIANS 3:12 NIV

My June 27th diary entry says, "Me, Brenda, and Mary went out to the mall and got our last names printed in black letters on the back of our softball T-shirts."

I can still remember how cool I felt. Finally, I had gotten on a team with my friends and we were proud of it. So proud, that we wanted to put our names on the back of our shirts.

We were chosen; we belonged.

That team and the feeling of belonging that went with it, only lasted a few brief weeks during that sweltering summer. But the belonging I have found in being God's chosen is lasting a lifetime.

"Chosen one."

This is exactly what Colossians 3:12 says that you are. You have been selected by God to be His one and it is a choosing that He will never change His mind about.

Because we are His, we have His name on the back of our shirts. We belong to Him. As His, God encourages us to put on His "jersey" of compassion, kindness, humility, gentleness, and patience. It's a choice we make to be like the One who has chosen us.

Every day when you wake up, you choose what to wear. That's the picture that Colossians 3:12 creates for us. God says that because we belong to Him, we are to put on compassion, kindness, humility, gentleness and patience. It's not a matter of if we feel like it. We do this because we are His.

Will you put on His jersey of love today so others can see to whom you belong?

LIVING CHERISHED

Who will you show these "Chosen One" traits to today? List their names here and pray about how they, too, can feel chosen.

....

....

....

TALKING WITH GOD

God, thank You for choosing me. Help me to make the choice to put on compassion, kindness, humility, gentleness, and patience . . . just like I chose to put on my shoes today. In Jesus' name, amen.

ARE YOU "ALL IN?"

LYNN

For I am sure that neither death nor life, nor angels nor rulers, nor things present nor things to come, nor powers, nor height nor depth, nor anything else in all creation, will be able to separate us from the love of God in Christ Jesus our Lord.

ROMANS 8:38–39 ESV

If I asked you to tell me about yourself, what things would you include?

Maybe the things you like and don't like, where you go to school, a bit about your family, your favorite thing to do on the weekend . . . and maybe that you are a Christian.

Listen to how God describes just how deep and powerful His love is for us: "For I am sure that neither death nor life, nor angels nor rulers, nor things present nor things to come, nor powers, nor height nor depth, nor anything else in all creation, will be able to separate us from the love of God in Christ Jesus our Lord" (Romans 8:38–39).

This is great news! There isn't *anything* that can remove God's love from us—nothing we do and nothing that happens to us.

When it comes to you and me, God is all in! He is giving His all to this relationship and has done all to be sure that nothing gets in the way of it. Knowing this makes me want to be all in as well; and let nothing in my life get in the way of it either.

This relationship we have with Him isn't something we pick and choose each day based on how we feel, where we're going, or what we might do. It's a connection between us and God that isn't just a part of our lives, it is our lives.

LIVING CHERISHED

How would you describe being "all in" in your relationship with God? Would you say that you are "all in?" If not, what do you want to do differently?

....

....

....

TALKING WITH GOD

Jesus, thank You that nothing can separate me from Your love. No matter what comes my way, help me to know this deep within. Thank You for being "all in." In Jesus' name, amen.

MORE AND MORE LIKE HIM

LYNN

So all of us who have had that veil removed can see and reflect the glory of the Lord. And the Lord—who is the Spirit—makes us more and more like him as we are changed into his glorious image.

2 CORINTHIANS 3:18 NLT

I have this habit that really isn't that great. When the news comes on the radio or TV, I usually turn it off. I know it is important to know what is happening in our world, but often, the things happening in our world are people hurting people. Hearing of this hurt makes me feel helpless to do anything about it.

I'm coming to realize, though, that becoming a part of the change that our world needs can take place with one small change at a time. And that is something I can be a part of!

A very wise man named Martin Luther King, Jr. said, "Darkness cannot drive out darkness; only light can do that. Hate cannot drive out hate; only love can do that."

When we see hateful actions, whether it's in our social media or in the halls at school, it's because love is not there. Love is not in the people who are doing the hurting. Have you ever heard, "Hurt people hurt people"? Pain and not knowing that they are immensely loved causes hurting people to hurt other people. I know it sounds backwards, but here's something encouraging.

You and I can be a part of turning it around!

As we learn how much God loves us, as 2 Corinthians 3:18 says, we become more and more like Jesus. God's love for us makes us brave to love people who are not like us.

When God's love is in us, people can see it. They see Jesus in us! Looking at us is like looking into a mirror and seeing God because God is in you and me.

This is the power that love has to change us. Not only is knowing we are loved and cherished good for us, it's good for the world. When we know who we are because of Jesus, we can share this only thing that will truly change our world. We change into people who are brave and can love others because we are becoming more like God, who is love. We become love, just like God is love.

LIVING CHERISHED

Think of someone (or a few people) you know who might not know they are unconditionally loved by God. Write their name(s) below. Pray now and over the next three days that they will know how much God loves them.

....

....

....

TALKING WITH GOD

God, thank You that You are changing me to reflect Your love to other people. Empower me to be brave. Show me one way that I can show _____ that they are loved by You. In Jesus' name, amen.

TREASURE INSIDE

LYNN

We now have this light shining in our hearts, but we ourselves are like fragile clay jars containing this great treasure. This makes it clear that our great power is from God, not from ourselves.

2 CORINTHIANS 4:7 NLT

If I looked in your closet, I imagine I'd find several shirts with words written across the front. They'd tell what team you play on, what play you were in, or where your family had its reunion last summer.

I wish I could send you a new T-shirt to add to your collection. It would say, "Treasure Inside."

See, not only are you loved and treasured, but you carry treasure *in* you!

You and I value some crazy things. Most of them are things we can lose or have taken from us: "likes" on social media, a place in the popular group, or the back-to-school outfit we just got. Then there's our purse, our backpack, our hair straightener, or phone.

The richest thing we truly have, though, is the treasure we carry *inside*.

This treasure is Love Himself—Jesus—the One who is wild about you! Because of this love you carry, there's also the light you carry. It's a result of His love in and for you. This love has power; the power to give you confidence, bravery, and the knowledge that you are deeply and forever loved.

This treasure inside you also has the power to bring life change to others as you share the love that has been shared with you. With God's power in you, you can boldly become a giver of love because you know how deeply you are loved.

Some people may act like they don't want this love, that they don't want Jesus. But just know, at some point in our lives, all people want to know that they are valued. They want to know they are cared about and cared for. When they come to that place, the love of Jesus that you have shone into their lives will be a light that is remembered.

LIVING CHERISHED

What is one way that you can shine the light of Jesus' love with someone today? Write it here and then come back and describe how it went.

....

....

....

TALKING WITH GOD

God, sometimes it's scary to love people, especially since the ones who seem to need it most can be the ones who are the hardest of all to love. Thank You that Your love and light in me is what they need, and it's not about me at all. In Jesus' name, amen.

DAY 95

LOVING OTHERS

Lynn

A new command I give you: Love one another. As I have loved you, so you must love one another.

JOHN 13:34 NIV

Did you learn to ride a bike? Maybe an adult plopped you on a two-wheeler, running alongside you as you wobbled and wiggled your way down the driveway. They stayed right there beside you until . . . you were doing it alone! Look at you go! Hair flying in the wind; you were riding a bike!

Learning something new usually doesn't just happen. You didn't climb up on that seat and know how to balance immediately. You didn't know how to tie your shoe the first time you tried or walk as soon as you learned to stand. You had no idea how to use a fork and spoon. All of these things were taught to you. Someone loved you and showed you how. First, they did it for you, then they helped you, and finally you learned how to do it yourself.

That's how it works with learning to love. Yes, we must learn to love. It doesn't always come naturally to us.

Jesus loved us first. He shows us what love looks like and how to love others.

Now He tells us that in the same way that He loves and treasures us, we are to love and treasure others. *This means everyone,* with no exceptions.

"A new command I give you: Love one another. As I have loved you, so you must love one another" (John 13:34).

Will it be easy? Was learning to multiply, roller blade, or swim easy? Sometimes we learn quickly and other times it's harder. Either way, we don't have to figure it out on our own. We are loved, and now, with the power of the Holy Spirit living in us, we can love others.

LIVING CHERISHED

What part of loving others do you think is easy? When is loving others hard?

....

....

....

TALKING WITH GOD

Jesus, I want to learn to love others, not because of what they do for me or even because I like them. Help me to love others because You have asked me to and because I love You. In Jesus' name, amen.

LABELED AS HIS

Lynn

In him you also, when you heard the word of truth, the gospel of your salvation, and believed in him, were sealed with the promised Holy Spirit,

EPHESIANS 1:13 ESV

In my refrigerator I have a brand-new bottle of my favorite hot sauce. (I like the type of toppings that do a little dance on my tongue!) This bottle has a seal that goes around the cap, put on by the makers of the hot sauce. The seal does several things.

First, the maker is the only one who has that seal, so I know when I buy it, it's not fake. It is the original recipe from the creator.

Second, the seal keeps the sauce inside safe from anyone messing with it before I get to pour it all over my tacos.

The seal on the bottle and the seal God puts on us as His children have some things in common. (I know it is a bit weird to compare God with my hot sauce but work with me here!)

When our Creator poured into us His love and His new life through Jesus, He put on us His seal. This seal is the Holy Spirit, the One who comes to live in us when we give our lives to Jesus.

Another version puts it this way: "And now you Gentiles have also heard the truth, the Good News that God saves you.

And when you believed in Christ, he identified you as his own by giving you the Holy Spirit, whom he promised long ago" (Ephesians 1:13 NLT).

The seal God gave you, His Holy Spirit living in you, identifies you as His. His Spirit in you also reminds you that because you are His, you are secure in Him. He has you, is with you, and will never leave you.

LIVING CHERISHED

Take a look in your pantry or refrigerator. Do any of the foods have seals on them? What other types of things can have seals that tell you what is inside or protects what is contained inside? Remember: His seal on you tells you that you are His.

....

....

....

TALKING WITH GOD

God, thank You for giving me the Holy Spirit as one way for me to know and remember that I am Yours. In Jesus' name, amen.

209

HE LISTENS

LYNN

O you who hear prayer, to you shall all flesh come.

PSALM 65:2 ESV

How would you define *prayer?*

When I was growing up, I would hear adults pray long prayers, using words we didn't use every day. It was almost like Christians had their own language. If you didn't know how to pray this way—with big, fancy words—then you'd better not pray out loud. At least that is what I thought sometimes.

But, when I was just talking to Jesus, I somehow knew I was talking to my friend. He was my safe place where I could share what I was happy about or what was causing me to feel sad. I even let Him know when I felt angry.

This is what prayer is—simply talking with Jesus. I've learned this from reading God's Word, especially the Psalms. David's conversations with God teach me that prayer is a conversation between you and the One who loves you. Psalm 65:2 says, "Everyone will come to you because you answer prayer" (CEV).

God actively listens and responds to us; He answers our prayers. He may not always answer the way we expect or the way we want, but one thing we do know—He doesn't ignore us.

LIVING CHERISHED

Read Matthew 6:9–13, which is a prayer that Jesus is praying to God. Look for the types of things He talks to His Father about and list them below.

....

....

....

TALKING WITH GOD

God, thank You for not making prayer difficult. I want to learn to talk with You all day in any place, knowing that I can come to You and You will answer my prayer in Your way. In Jesus' Name, amen.

NEVER CHANGING

LYNN

*You will seek me and find me when you
seek me with all your heart.*

JEREMIAH 29:13 NIV

Every day you are changing. You might look in the mirror before you go to bed and see one image. But when you look in the morning, something's different. You might have a pimple that wasn't there yesterday. You might notice parts of your body growing that weren't growing before! *Everything is changing.* It might be changing faster than you want, or you might be wondering what's taking so long!

While all of this change is happening, there's Someone who is constant and will never change: God.

From the time you said yes to becoming His, He became your promise-keeping, protective Father. He has been and always will be the Father who is with you and always will be . . . no matter what. The more we understand who He is, how absolutely wonderful and grand He is, the more we'll understand who we are because we are loved by Him!

This is why getting to know Him is so important. God tells us just *how* to discover who He is.

Jeremiah 29:13 tells us, "You will seek me and find me when you seek me with all your heart."

I once lost my cell phone. (Once? That's not really true. I lose it often!) When I can't find something important, I will go to any extreme to find it. I have to! It's important to me.

That's how God wants us to be when it comes to seeking and finding Him. He wants us to seek Him—to go in search of Him and then try to discover who He is and what He's like. We do that by reading His Word and asking questions. As we do, we learn more and more about Him and oh, do we have a lot to learn!

The best thing of all: As I learn what God is like, it helps me better understand who I am because I am His.

LIVING CHERISHED

What is changing about you right now? Are you looking forward to change? Remind yourself that no matter what changes, God never will.

....

....

....

TALKING WITH GOD

God, I know I have a lot to learn about You. It gives me comfort to know that no matter what I learn about You from Your Word, it won't change tomorrow because You never change. In Jesus' name, amen.

GIVE IT AWAY

LYNN

By this all people will know that you are my
disciples, if you have love for one another.
JOHN 13:35 ESV

If I draw a swoosh like a checkmark right here, would you know what it stands for? Yep, Nike. An apple with a bite out of the side? Sure . . . Apple. What about five circles—three on top and two on the bottom? The Olympics.

These symbols are so well known to us, we don't even have to use words. People all around the world know what we are referring to, even if we don't speak the same language.

One reason it's so important for us to understand that we are loved and cherished is because those around us need to know that they are loved and cherished too.

When you wear shoes with a swoosh on the side, people know Nike made them. When you use a phone with an apple on the back, it identifies the maker of the phone.

When you love people—all people, regardless of how much they are like you or are different from you—you show people Jesus.

Jesus' label, or symbol, is love. He chooses to use words to communicate His love in the Bible, but words have no meaning or power unless they are backed up with actions.

The same is true with us. We can say that we love people, but there needs to be actions to prove it's true. When you include the person who looks different from you, you are showing Jesus' love. When you are respectful to the rude kid at school, your actions display Jesus' love. Inviting the loner to sit by you at lunch, choosing the slower one for your team, or texting an invitation to the unpopular girl . . . these actions show Jesus' love. When you and I do things that display love, we show them Jesus. We are the very thing that causes others to want to know our Jesus.

This is what happens when we know we are loved and cherished; it changes us. It makes us different and others will know that we are His.

LIVING CHERISHED

In the space below, write out one action you can take, without using words, that shows someone who doesn't know Jesus His love.

....

....

....

TALKING WITH GOD

Jesus, saying "I love you" is a lot easier than actually showing love. I want this knowledge that I am loved and cherished to not just change me, but to change the life of someone else because of the love pouring out of me. In Jesus' name, amen.

ON YOUR OWN

Lynn

*Therefore, my beloved, as you have always
obeyed, so now, not only as in my presence
but much more in my absence, work out your
own salvation with fear and trembling.*

PHILIPPIANS 2:12 ESV

You are in a new season of life, gaining new privileges and responsibilities every day! But there are still a few things you aren't able to do on your own. You can't drive to get ice cream when you want. You might not be able to decide if you want to keep your room tidy or a bit messy.

Here is something you can do on your own: work on your relationship with God. The great thing about our relationship with God is that it isn't dependent on any other relationship. If your mom doesn't have a relationship with Jesus, that doesn't mean you can't have one. If your dad, your grandma, your schoolteacher, or your neighbor isn't close to Him, that doesn't mean you can't be close to God.

Some people might think Philippians 2:12 is confusing, but I really like it. It says, "Therefore, my beloved, as you have always obeyed, so now, not only as in my presence but much more in my absence, work out your own salvation with fear and trembling."

Paul, who wrote this verse, is telling the Philippians, "It's time for you to learn to walk on your own instead of leaning too much on me." Paul has been their spiritual father, but he is now encouraging them to take responsibility and grow in their relationship with God on their own.

I want to do that with you. We've been together for many days now . . . walking together to learn more about Jesus and His great love for you.

Now I want you to picture me placing your hand directly into Jesus' hands and saying to you, "You and Jesus . . . you two have got this together!"

He is so excited to meet with you! I hope you are just as excited to meet with Him!

LIVING CHERISHED

I want to challenge you to read a book of the Bible completely on your own. You might start with John; the story of Jesus' life here on Earth. You could also start with a letter like 1 John. I know that might sound overwhelming, but remember, the more you read and learn about God, the closer you'll get to Him. If you get stuck or feel something is too hard to understand, ask someone you know for some help. That's what I do. Write out a few ideas of books to start with, and then pick one from your list.

....

....

....

TALKING WITH GOD

God, I am ready to start digging into Your Word, just You and me. Teach me, Holy Spirit, the things I need to know as I am growing to love You more. In Jesus' name, amen.

WHAT IT MEANS TO FOLLOW JESUS

God loves you so very much and wants you to have a joy-filled, peaceful, and full life! That life only comes one way; through His Son, Jesus.

Romans 5:1 NLT puts it this way: "Therefore, since we have been made right in God's sight by faith, we have peace with God because of what Jesus Christ our Lord has done for us."

A lot of people don't have that joy-filled, peaceful life, do they? Why is that?

It is because we have sin in our lives that has separated us from God. Romans 3:23 NLT says, "For everyone has sinned; we all fall short of God's glorious standard."

That is why Jesus had to come to earth. He is God's perfect Son. He was the only one who could take away our sin; the only one who could pay the price to wipe away the sin in our lives. "Christ suffered for our sins once for all time. He never sinned, but he died for sinners to bring you safely home to God. He suffered physical death, but he was raised to life in the Spirit" (1 Peter 3:18 NLT).

Our response, then, is to receive this gift of forgiveness that Jesus offers to us. He describes this invitation in Revelation 3:20 NLT: "Look! I stand at the door and knock. If you hear my voice and open the door, I will come in, and we will share a meal together as friends."

So, to begin this new life with Jesus we need to:

1. Agree with God that we are sinners.
2. Determine that we don't want to choose our own way to live anymore.
3. Believe that Jesus is the only way our sins can be forgiven.
4. Ask Him to forgive us and give Him our lives.

Would you like to do this? Begin a new life with Jesus? Then you can pray this prayer:

Dear Jesus, I am a sinner in need of a Savior. Please forgive me for my sin. Take it away and give me a new life in You. I give you control of my life and will live for You and with You forever. In Jesus' name, Amen.

Loved and Cherished Online Resource

In today's cultural environment, a young girl finds herself continually in a position of evaluation. *Am I loved? Am I valuable? Am I smart? Am I pretty? Am I …* The questions can go on for as long as her imagination and insecurities allow. These insecurities being developed in her life can come from sources such as social media and social pressures, but they can even come from parental pressure or absence. A girl needs to know that she is enough because of God's love and she is loved exactly for who she is, even if she doesn't change a thing.

Now is the time in a girl's life when she needs to have women come around her to build a firm foundation of love so she can withstand the pressures that only mount as she grows older. The *Loved & Cherished* study guide is a partner resource designed to be experienced in a group setting such as a Bible study, Sunday School class, or any small group gathering. It can also be used one-on-one with a mentor and mentee or mother/daughter.

Loaded with ice breakers, discussion questions, and prayer guides, this resource takes all of the guesswork out of leading girls to know they are loved and cherished.

Loved & Cherished equips girls ages 8–12 to:

- Discover perfect love in God, even if she has not experienced unconditional love.
- Know she has His protection, despite living in an often-scary world.
- Reduce her fear of the future, for she has the love she needs to face it.
- Recognize God's love as the source to heal her from life's heartaches.
- Build her faith on the love who will never leave her.

Loved & Cherished helps prepare girls for the temptation to build her worth on the affections that will be offered to her on various levels in her near future. It will empower the middle-grade girl to find love, acceptance, and approval from God's love that is sure, stable, and secure. It will also help her to build an understanding that finding security (something she might not even know that she desires or needs yet) comes from understanding God's love for her.

Loved & Cherished addresses the undermining and beginning stages of seeking people's approval, which can lead to various harmful choices. This approval may be something she's never thought of before, yet it can be gained as she is introduced to God's love and discovers the love that gives her the foundation to be strong and secure.

Find this study guide at www.lovedandcherished.me.

Brave Beauty
Finding the Fearless You

Lynn Cowell

100 courage-building moments to help girls 8–12 explore who they are, easing their fears and anxiety, while inspiring them to strive toward the woman they want to be through this exciting yet confusing season of change.

From Proverbs 31 Ministries speaker and blogger, Lynn Cowell, comes Faithgirlz' *Brave Beauty: Finding the Fearless You*. These 100 motivating moments guide tween girls to reflect on Scripture and find confidence in God, rather than in someone, some place, or something, as pop culture is telling them.

Throughout these pages—formatted as theme-based mini chapters that can be read once a day, once a week, or at the reader's own pace—Lynn prepares tween girls to:

- Overcome confidence-defeating thoughts and stand on who Jesus says she is.
- Build a strong foundation to face the fickle, sometimes hurtful opinions of others.
- Find approval of herself even when she lacks the acceptance of others.
- Walk confidently through the exciting, yet scary world of growing up by turning to Christ step by step.

Featuring a gorgeous, foil decorated hardcover and beautifully formatted pages modeled after the well-known and loved Faithgirlz brand of books, Lynn's relatable, conversational tone makes it easy for girls to feel like they're in a safe place spending time with a close friend.

Available in stores and online!

Now Hear This!

Have you found the message of *Loved & Cherished* to be one you would like to bring to your community for a live event? Lynn and Michelle would love to partner with you to invest in the girls and women in your community, empowering them to better understand, know, and experience the life-changing love of God. To learn more, please stop by their websites at:

https://lynncowell.com/speaking/

http://michellenietert.com/

Proverbs 31
MINISTRIES

Know the Truth. Live the Truth.
It changes everything.

If you were inspired by *Loved and Cherished* and desire to deepen your own personal relationship with Jesus Christ, Proverbs 31 Ministries has just what you are looking for.

Proverbs 31 Ministries exists to be a trusted friend who will take you by the hand and walk by your side, leading you one step closer to the heart of God through:

- Free online daily devotions
- First 5 Bible study app
- Online Bible Studies
- Podcast
- COMPEL Writer Training
- She Speaks Conference
- Books and resources

Our desire is to help you to know the Truth and live the Truth. Because when you do, it changes everything.

For more information about Proverbs 31 Ministries, visit:

www.Proverbs31.org.